100
WAYS TO TELL
God's
Great
Story

PHYLLIS VOS WEZEMAN

To Adelaide Ortegal and Cathy Campbell...

...Thank you for telling THE story in so many ways and for sharing YOUR stories with our family. P.V.W.

100 Ways to Tell God's Great Story

ISBN 0-687-33443-8

Art by Barbara Ball
Page 5: Megan Jeffrey; Pages 14, 24: Florence Davis, ©2001 Abingdon Press; Page 42: Robert S. Jones

06 07 08 09 10 11 12 13 14 15—10 9 8 7 6 5 4 3 2 1
MANUFACTURED IN THE UNITED STATES OF AMERICA

TABLE OF CONTENTS

TABLE OF CONTENTS CONTINUED

INTRODUCTION

"I love to tell the story!" The words of the favorite old hymn say it well. Throughout the centuries the church has told of God's love through the medium of the story. Storytelling has been, and continues to be, an integral part of of every congregation's ministries of worship, education, and nurture.

ONE HUNDRED WAYS TO TELL GOD'S GREAT STORY is a book that offers more than one hundred ways to tell *the* story. It is a collection of multidimensional approaches to learning. Each chapter focuses on a different method: Architecture, Art—Art Techniques, Art—Drawing and Painting, Creative Writing, Creative Writing—Poetry, Culinary, Games—Game Formats, Games—Sequencing Games, Music, and Puppetry. Each chapter, or method, contains ten suggestions/techniques to help children, and adults, discover and develop ways to use the activities to learn Old Testament and New Testament stories. Even though specific examples might be suggested, in general each of the methods may be adapted to any story.

Provided in an easy-to-use format, each suggestion is organized into two parts—materials and method. "Materials," which appears in the side columns, lists the required supplies. "Method" contains directions for accomplishing the task.

Ideas in ONE HUNDRED WAYS TO TELL GOD'S GREAT STORY are intended to supplement existing curricula, but they may also be used for a special emphasis on a particular way of learning. For example, you are teaching the story of Jesus' birth. What are some ways you can teach the story through the eyes of his mother, Mary? How can you help your students appreciate the thrill and challenge of God's plan for Mary's life—and for their lives, as well? That's the point at which this book becomes an extremely helpful resource.

Review the ten techniques presented in this book and look at the specific options that would be helpful to use. For example, creative writing might be an appropriate way to reflect upon God's plan for each person's life, or a breath painting might be created to convey the message.

The techniques in this resource can also be used to open, enrich, expand, or conclude any lesson when a teacher needs five or ten minutes of ideas to adapt the class schedule. This book can be used as an extension for enhancing, as well as for planning lessons.

Do you have a midweek ministry? Are you free to select a story based on the season of the church year or on the focus of a particular program? Once you know the focus for a lesson, what is next? Effective teachers know that a lesson has key elements that guide student learning from the introduction of an objective to a meaningful outcome. Effective teachers plan each lesson carefully and intentionally, much like an accomplished cook plans a balanced menu from appetizer to dessert.

For example, you want to focus on the stories of the meals Jesus shared with his followers. The first story is "The Feeding of the Five Thousand." You want an interactive approach to the story to convey the importance of offering our gifts to God, just as the little boy offered the five loaves and the two fish to feed the crowd.

To find something catchy to introduce the lesson and the objectives, sift through the chapters contained in this book.

- An idea in the chapter on "Telling the Story Through Music" may inspire you to write simple words to a familiar tune to introduce the message and the sequence of the miracle God gave by the Sea of Galilee.
- Next you might select a sequencing game as a method to review an eyewitness account of the miracle.
- To review the critical concept, you could choose a creative writing approach, contrasting the words *hungry* and *fed*.
- As closure, you could ask your students to draw a picture of a gift that they can give to God.

The beauty of this book is that no matter the teaching situation and no matter the lesson assigned, you can use and re-use the contents to find a fresh approach to telling the story—and ultimately, to help the learners make it their story. Jesus used storytelling as his primary teaching tool. He improvised the lesson based on his listeners and their needs. While none of us can expect to teach like the Master, we can adopt a more flexible approach that allows creativity and innovation to guide our lesson preparation and presentation.

While the activities in ONE HUNDRED WAYS TO TELL GOD'S GREAT STORY are mainly intended for learners in a classroom, they may be easily adapted for use by children, youth, and adults in small-group and large-group settings. They are ideal for religious education classes, parochial school programs, vacation Bible school courses, confirmation sessions, intergenerational events, youth groups, retreat settings, family devotions, home schooling, and more.

May each person who uses this resource find many ways to share biblical stories, contemporary stories, historical stories, and personal stories in order to claim God's story as his or her own.

TELLING THE STORY THROUGH ARCHITECTURE

Architecture is an important, but often overlooked, medium to use as a method for introducing children to and involving them in biblical stories and themes. Explore architecture to build new awareness of both short-term and long-term possibilities for projects and programs. Ten ideas for using this teaching tool are provided.

BRIDGE

METHOD

A bridge may be a huge architectural structure that spans a major body of water, or a modest board placed over a small stream to join two pieces of dry ground. Regardless of its size, its function is to connect two areas and to enable people to get from one place to another.

Show the students pictures of bridges, or build one out of wooden blocks or connecting blocks. Talk about the ways in which "bridges" were needed in families in Bible times, as well as the ways that "bridges" are needed in families today. Share an example such as the Old Testament story of Jacob and Esau or various accounts of David and his sons. Help the children think of some of the bridges that were needed in these situations. Brainstorm words such as *communication, honesty, imagination, knowledge*, and *support*. Help them understand that these same "bridges" are needed in families today.

Post a large sheet of newsprint on a wall or bulletin board, and draw the ends of a bridge on each side of the paper. Ask the children to work together to connect the two sides by writing on the paper the "bridge-building" words they just thought of, or by drawing pictures of these ideas on the sheet.

MATERIALS
Bible(s)
wooden or
  connecting
  blocks
markers
paper or newsprint
pictures of bridges
tape

7

DOOR

MATERIALS

Bible(s)
crayons or
  markers
dictionary
door
roll of paper such
  as mural paper
  or newsprint; or
  plastic tablecloth
scissors
tape
optional: catalogs
  or magazines

METHOD

In advance, cover a door with paper. Depending on the size of the group, one or both sides of the door may be used. Print the word *WELCOME* vertically down the center of the paper.

As the participants arrive, invite them to gather around the door of the room. Greet each person individually. Encourage the children to welcome one another. After everyone has assembled, use the dictionary to look up the meaning of the word *welcome*: "a manner of greeting someone in a friendly way." Talk about times and places where the participants have felt welcomed and about situations when they did not feel welcomed.

Next, look up the meaning of the word *door* in the dictionary. One definition is a "means of access." Explain that a door is often associated with the word *welcome*, since it can be opened or closed to people. Use the door to list things people can do to make another person feel welcome. The words or phrases can begin with or include the letters of the word *welcome*. Children can write their own words and phrases directly on the door; young children can draw pictures of their ideas, or they can suggest words and themes, and a leader can write them on the door.

Before beginning the project, brainstorm a few words or phrases to use, such as *call, eat*, and *wave*. Provide markers or crayons. Pictures may also be cut from magazines and added to the door. Review the results of the project together.

Conclude by reminding the class that Jesus welcomed children, as well as all people. In John 10:9, Jesus said, "I am the gate," which can be understood as the "door" to eternal life.

LANDSCAPING MATERIALS

METHOD

Use landscape architecture as a way to help children reflect on things shared by people throughout the world. Since the landscaping around many places of worship and schools often contains plants, shrubs, trees, and flowers that originate in various countries, create a miniature international garden by labeling each part in some attractive way. Invite someone from a landscaping service to speak to the students and to help them identify where some of the vegetation on their grounds is found in the world. Also prepare a diagram of the premises to help people locate different plants and to identify the plants' countries of origin.

As an alternative, modify the plan to help the children create a biblical garden or a prayer garden on the church grounds.

MATERIALS

resource
  materials on
  plants
paper
marker
landscaping labels

MODEL

METHOD

Hospitality is a theme that the Apostle John emphasizes in all fifteen verses of his Third Epistle. Hospitality, an essential Christian practice, involves welcoming people—family, friends, and even strangers—into our hearts and into our homes. It may involve gathering for a visit, offering a place to sleep, or sharing a meal. John reminds his New Testament readers, as well as Christians today, that we share God's love when we open our lives, as well as the place we live, to others through the practice of hospitality.

Depending on its location in the world, a home may be called a camper, a cave, a chalet, a cliff dwelling, or a cottage. Throughout the seven continents, the types of homes in which people reside are as varied as their inhabitants; however, all houses have several things in common. Homes provide shelter and security for people. And they should also be a place to offer hospitality to others.

Explore various types of homes found throughout the world and build models of several of them. Start the project by looking at illustrations and photographs, as well as models or videos, of homes in various parts of the world. Besides books and magazines, an excellent resource to use for this activity is the children's story, *People*, a spectacularly illustrated picture book by Peter Spier. It contains two large pages depicting twenty-five types of homes found throughout the world.

MATERIALS

Bible(s)
cardboard
fabric scraps
glue
markers
materials for
  constructing
  models of homes
paper
People (Spier,
  Peter. Doubleday
  Books for Young
  Readers, 1980)
resource
  materials on
  types of homes
  throughout the
  world
rope
scissors
tape
wood scraps

For an individual activity, have each participant choose one country and make a model of one type of home found in that particular place. Use a variety of supplies for the project and construct a representation of a type of dwelling typical in a certain area of the world. For a cooperative project, work together to create the model homes. Organize into two or more teams and select a country and a type of home for each group. For example, Team One might be told to make a reed house from Bolivia, Team Two a *jhuggi* from India, and Team Three a villa from Italy.

Use the format of a relay race to build the model homes from the materials provided. Designate a construction site for each team that contains basic supplies such as glue, scissors, string, and tape. Place the miscellaneous materials such as cardboard, fabric, paper, rope, and wood on a table at one end of the room. Have the teams stand at the opposite end of the space. When the leader says "Go," the first person on each team runs to the other side of the room, takes an item from the table, and returns to the group's construction site. Each player is to select one item that he or she thinks will help make a good model. That item is added to the home the team is building. Continue until each player has had a turn. If necessary, repeat the process until enough materials are gathered for the models.

When time is up, or when the models are completed, have each team display its newly created home. Gather the models to form a large collage that can be displayed in a prominent place in the congregation, school, or community.

PROJECT

information on Habitat for Humanity

METHOD

Habitat for Humanity is an international organization with many local chapters that rehabilitates older houses and builds new homes for people who cannot afford adequate housing.

Invite a speaker to describe Habitat's program and to challenge participants to become involved in a local, neighborhood project.

SCULPTURE

METHOD

In the Book of Colossians, the Apostle Paul makes an important point: Each believer is connected to God through Jesus, and to other Christians through the body of Christ—the church. Although this message is the emphasis of the author's New Testament Epistle, it is also the point of every book of the Bible. In order to make this connection, create a toothpick sculpture to illustrate the way that all Christians are connected to Christ. Begin by printing the name of each person in the class, or in several classes, on a slip of paper. Glue or tape each name to a separate toothpick.

MATERIALS
Bible(s)
glue or tape
plastic-based clay
posterboard
scissors
slips of paper
toothpicks
wax paper

Place a sheet of wax paper over the work surface. Roll the plastic-based clay into several one-fourth to one-half inch balls. Insert the point of a toothpick (with an attached name), into a ball of clay. Then connect the opposite end of the toothpick to another ball of clay. Continue connecting toothpicks with the clay balls until all have been used. Place the finished project on a piece of posterboard to display the sculpture.

STAINED GLASS

METHOD

MATERIALS

page 14
Bible(s)
9- by 12-inch
  black
  construction
  paper
glue sticks or
  rubber cement
pencils
scissors
exacto knives
tape
tissue or crepe
  paper
various colors
trays or boxes
wax paper

In advance, cut tissue or crepe paper sheets into smaller sections, and place the pieces in a shirt box or tray. Have sheets of black construction paper available. Also cut pieces of wax paper a little smaller than the pieces of black paper you are using. Photocopy page 14 for each student.

Many of the most magnificent stained-glass windows appear in cathedrals and churches throughout the world. Stained-glass windows were intended not only to beautify, but also to instruct. Before Scripture was readily available in print, parishioners were taught by studying visual images and lessons in the architecture of the church building. Show the children the symbols that represent the Trinity, such as a shamrock, three entwined circles, or a triangle, that they may have seen in stained glass windows. (See the top of page 14.).

Have the children cut out the larger pattern of the entwined circles. Have them use exacto knives to cut out the open spaces. Then have them trace the design onto black paper and cut it out. Have them flip the paper framework over and begin gluing colored paper pieces to the open areas. Use glue or narrow tape strips to fasten the colors to the black paper. Arrange vivid colors to simulate stained glass. When all the open areas are filled with color, glue or tape on a backing of wax paper to strengthen the window. Have them trim carefully so that the wax paper does not show around the edges on the front of the stained glass. The stained-glass designs will glow with color when displayed in a window that allows light to show through.

STRUCTURES

METHOD

MATERIALS

pictures of places
  of worship
  related to world
  religions

As a way to show children how the beliefs of a congregation influence the architecture of its building, take a field trip by foot, car, bus, or picture. Visit historic congregations and religious institutions from various faith traditions in the area. Or show the children pictures of other places of worship.

Arrange to have someone in each place talk with the children about the building's and the believers' backgrounds. Note how the structure was designed and built to reflect the religious heritage of its original worshipers. Point out ways that this is depicted in the architecture.

TOUR

METHOD

Help the children identify and illustrate the unique structural aspects of their church. If possible, obtain and show the blueprints for the building. Then tour the interior of the facility. Name the architectural features in the process, including the baptismal font, chancel, choir loft, Communion table, pews, pulpit, and so forth.

When the group returns to the classroom, provide paper and pencils or pens, and offer an opportunity for the children to make their own drawings of the various parts of the worship space. Suggest that they write captions to describe the illustrations.

MATERIALS
blueprints
paper
pencils or pens

WALL

METHOD

Show the children a picture of the Wailing Wall in Jerusalem. Tell the group that the wall is from the second temple that was built by the Jews. About seventy years after Jesus' death, the temple was destroyed, and all that was left is this section of the West Wall. For many centuries, people have come to the wall to pray. Many lament the destruction of Jerusalem and pray for its restoration. They also pray about the sad and happy things in their lives.

Invite the children to make a temporary wall to use for prayer concerns. Offer each person one or more bricks to use to construct the wall. Explain that one of the customs of people who go to the Wailing Wall in Jerusalem is to write a prayer concern or request on a piece of paper and to place the paper into the cracks in the wall. Offer each participant a piece of paper and a pencil or a pen. Invite him or her to write a prayer on the paper and to place the paper into the wall.

MATERIALS
Bible(s)
bricks
paper
paper cutter or
  scissors
pencils or pens
picture(s) of the
  Wailing Wall in
  Jerusalem from
  the Internet or
  resource books

Trinity Stained-Glass Patterns

 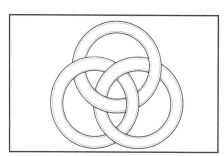 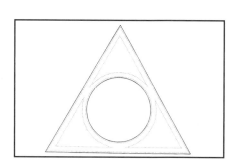

TELLING THE STORY THROUGH ART: ART TECHNIQUES

It's a good thing there are lots of Bible stories to tell: There are so many art techniques to use to teach them! Any art method, such as papier mâché or plaster molding, pottery or printmaking, can be used to recite, review, or reinforce a story.

The ten ideas presented in this chapter are only a starting point. Numerous other art methods should be incorporated into lesson preparation and presentation. For example, a rebus story activity might suggest drawing illustrations to represent words in the narrative; a creative writing exercise could recommend having the learners make a collage of their reactions and responses; and a puppetry project may direct the group to paint interesting characters, props, and scenery. Regardless of the method used, try telling the story through art.

COLLAGE

METHOD

Make a wax paper heart as a reminder of God's faithful love for God's people then and now—the heart of the message of the Bible.

Use the pattern on page 23 as a guide to cut two large heart shapes from wax paper. Tear or cut small pieces approximately one inch square out of tissue paper. Print information about the Scripture passage, story, or verse on each piece.

Glue the tissue pieces onto one sheet of wax paper in an overlapping design. Lay the other heart on top. Using an iron set on warm, push the iron once over the double heart to fuse the two pieces together with the tissue squares in between. Use the stained-glass heart to share the message of God's love.

MATERIALS
page 23
glue sticks
iron
scissors
tissue paper
wax paper

DOUGH FIGURES

MATERIALS

acrylic paints
aluminum foil
baking trays
Bible(s)
all-purpose flour
measuring
  utensils
mixing bowls
oven
paintbrushes
salt
toothpicks
water

METHOD

In the Book of Ephesians one of the most important themes to remember is that even though each of Jesus' followers are distinctive people, we are all one in Christ. And even though each Christian has been given different gifts, we are all one in the Spirit and are to use our talents and our time to build up the body of Christ, the church. Demonstrate this important truth by making a unique collection of dough people. It might be necessary to form the figures in one session, bake them after class, and decorate them another week.

To make dough for about twelve figures, combine three cups of all-purpose flour, one cup of salt, and one cup of water in a mixing bowl. Knead the dough until it is smooth and rubbery. For each figure, form a head by rolling a piece of dough between the palms. It should be roughly the size of a Ping-Pong ball.

Make a second slightly larger ball for the torso. Or to dress the figure in a skirt, shape a triangular trunk. Press the head onto the torso, applying a few drops of water to make the dough sticky, if necessary. Next, shape and attach cylindrical arms and legs.

Pinch the lower ends of the legs to form feet. Attach ears and a nose and use a toothpick to etch facial features. Bake the figures on a foil-lined cookie sheet for one hour in a 275-degree oven. Remove the tray(s) from the oven and set them aside until cool enough to handle.

Decorate the figures with acrylic paints. Add facial features as well as clothing. Set the unique collection of people on a table to form a display.

METAL TOOLING

ADVANCE PREPARATION

Photocopy the Budded Cross pattern on page 24. Cut copper foil to match the pattern's size. Cut wood or mat board bases slightly larger than the copper rectangles.

METHOD

In the first chapter of the Book of Romans, Paul declares his main theme: [The gospel] is the power of salvation to everyone who has faith... (Romans 1:16-17). Paul goes on further to say that a response to our belief should be the sacrifice of one's entire life to the gospel. Romans 12:9-21 helps us know the Christian way of life.

The Budded Cross is used as a symbol for either the young or the new Christian. When we see a bud on a flower stem or a tree, we know that a more mature leaf or plant will soon follow. The buds on the Budded Cross represent those young in the Christian faith who hold a promise of full "growth."

Design a Budded Cross plaque using a process known as metal tooling. Select a piece of copper foil. Tape the corners of the cross pattern to the copper piece so the image will not shift. Place the pattern and copper on a magazine or a pad of newspaper. Trace all of the lines by pressing hard with an embossing stylus or pencil that has a dull point. Remove the paper design and go over the same outline directly on the metal.

Place the traced design face down on the pad and begin the embossing process. Use the "spoon" end of the special modeling tool or the bowl of a small spoon to press over all of the parts that will be raised in relief. Turn the piece right side up, move to a hard surface, and continue the process by rubbing around the cross to smooth the background away from the relief shape. Pushing into the pad allows for the metal sheet to stretch; pressing over the copper on a hard surface flattens bumps and ripples. Continue working on both sides of the metal until the design is clearly defined. Use care not to push in the raised image while smoothing the background area.

For a bright finish, polish the copper with steel wool and apply lacquer to maintain the shine.

Center the metal piece on the wooden or mat board base and tack it in place with a hammer and tiny pins or staples. Attach a picture hanger to the back of the base.

MATERIALS
page 24
Bible(s)
clear lacquer
copper tooling
  foil or other
  heavy-duty foil
utility knives
fine steel wool
pencil stubs
empty ballpoint
  pens and plastic
  or wooden
  spoons
magazines or
  newspapers
pencils
picture hangers
rags
scissors
tack hammer or
  stapler
tape
wood pieces or
  heavy mat
  boards
dowel rods or
  wooden styluses
embossing stylus

MOSAIC

MATERIALS

colorful magazine
  pages, tissue
  paper, and
  various types of
  paper
9- by 12-inch
  construction
  paper
glue and glue
  brushes or glue
  sticks
pictures of early
  Christian or
  contemporary
  mosaics
rulers
scissors
paper cutter
plastic foam trays
  or pie pans
toothpicks

ADVANCE PREPARATION

Use a pencil and ruler, or paper cutter, to cut paper into half-inch squares. Place the paper squares in pans or trays.

METHOD

Connect a symbol to a Bible story or verse and create a paper mosaic design to remember the theme. Mosaic is a form of embellishment that uses small pieces of glass, colorful stones, or bits of ceramic fastened into mortar or plaster. The small pieces are called "tesserae" and fit together to form a picture. Mosaics are most often used to decorate ceilings, walls, or floors inside buildings, but can also be used for courtyards and exterior walls. Many times mosaics portray information from Scripture.

Make a sample of mosaic design by cutting and gluing small squares of pre-cut paper into a background. Trace one of the symbol shapes associated with the story onto construction paper. Brush glue over a small area, and then place paper bits close together on the glued surface. The toothpicks will make it easier to move the paper squares. Continue until the design is filled in.

Finish the design by framing it with a border of pieces fit carefully around the edge of the background paper. Experiment with different papers and vary the sizes of tesserae. Display the mosaics in a hallway or on a bulletin board.

PAPER CUTTING

METHOD

Gospel is a word that means "Good News." The four Gospels—Matthew, Mark, Luke, and John—record the good news of the birth, life, death, and resurrection of Jesus. Construct a puzzle to remember the message of the Gospels.

Take four 3- by 5-inch index cards and trim one inch from the short end of two cards. Stack the trimmed and untrimmed cards, and then cut a point on one end of all four pieces at the same time. A ninety-degree angle will work best. Copy the name of each of the four Gospels on a separate section of the puzzle. Arrange the pieces with the points touching in the center; be sure to place the longer sections with points together and then fit in shorter cards. This symbol, the cross, is a reminder of the message of the Gospels: Jesus is the Savior. The Gospels make it clear that Jesus' death on the cross was part of God's plan to save us from our sins.

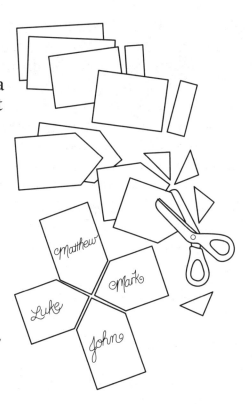

MATERIALS
Bible(s)
3-by-5 index
  cards
pencils
markers
scissors

PRINTING

METHOD

After the invention of the printing press, the first complete book known to be printed in the western world was the Bible in 1456. To remember that printing is an important part of the process of making a Bible, create a simple printing press. Use shoe insoles to create stamps. Insoles are made from a thin layer of foam with a layer of latex on top. Some insoles have adhesive backing on one side. Decide on a design to use for the project. It could be a word—such as *BIBLE*—or a symbol such as a heart. Draw the outline on the latex side of the insole and cut it out with scissors. Attach the adhesive backing to a wooden block, a metal jar lid, or an empty film can, or glue the foam in place. Press the printer onto an inked stamp pad and try the design on paper.

MATERIALS
pens
scissors
shoe insoles
  (adhesive
  backed, if
  possible)
scrap paper
stamp pads
wooden blocks,
  metal jar lids, or
  empty film cans

RUBBING

METHOD

MATERIALS

page 23
aluminum foil
chalk, crayons, or
  wax for rubbing
construction
  paper
glue
heart-shaped
  objects
masking tape
paper like onion
  skin, parchment,
  rice paper, or
  shelf paper
scissors

Every book of the Bible reminds us of God's steadfast love for God's people—through all time and for all time. If God is first in our hearts, our choices will reflect our love for God; and everything we do, say, and think will honor God.

Create a rubbing of a heart as a reminder to put God first in life and to demonstrate love for God through actions and attitudes. A rubbing is similar to a tracing; however, the finished design has a three-dimensional look. Photocopy and cut out the heart pattern on page 23. Place a piece of paper over the heart. Tape the edges down to keep the paper from slipping. Rub with the flat side of the crayon or other material. Move the crayon across the textured area with firm pressure and enough strokes to reveal the entire design. Experiment with different papers and rubbing materials. For an interesting variation, press aluminum foil over the design. Gently rub fingers over and around the raised or engraved areas. Display the rubbings just as they are, or cut out and arrange the most interesting textures into a heart-shaped collage.

SCULPTURE

METHOD

MATERIALS

Bible(s)
chenille stems,
  five per person
construction paper
cotton
foil wrap or
  tissue paper
glue
pencils or pens
ribbon
scissors
shallow
  containers such
  as margarine
  tubs
plastic foam

Share information about a Bible story, such as Pentecost, in the form of a *stabile*—a type of sculpture that has small parts that are fastened into a base.

To create the stabile, select construction paper—the same or different colors—to use to record the five *W* information about the account. Using pencil or pen, draw five shapes that are proportionate to the size of the base of a shallow container. Cut two identical pieces for each shape. Print each of the words—*Who, What, When, Where*, and *Why*—on two of the same shapes. Add additional information to fill the space.

Select five chenille stems. Place glue on the back side of one shape. Set a chenille stem on the wet surface, with two-thirds protruding from the bottom. Position the identical shape, writing side out, on top. For a three-dimensional look, place a small bit of cotton around the chenille stem before attaching the identical *W* word to the shape. Continue until all of the shapes are attached to the chenille stems. Set aside.

Pick a container to use as the base of the stabile. Cut a piece of plastic foam to fit inside of the container. Glue it to the bottom of the base. Stick each chenille stem into the core. It may be necessary to trim the stems to various lengths to add variety to the sculpture. To make the base more attractive, cover it with foil wrap or tissue paper and tie a piece of ribbon around the material to keep it in place.

THREE-DIMENSIONAL PEEK BOX

METHOD

MATERIALS
Bible(s)
black or gray
  paint
cardboard strips
chunks of coal or
  rocks
cloth scraps
construction
  paper
crayons
duct tape
figures from
  Sunday school
leaflets
fine-tipped
  markers
glue
paintbrushes
pencils
chenille stems
scissors or craft
  knives
shoeboxes
tissue paper and
  cellophane,
  flame colors

Nebuchadnezzar ordered Shadrach, Meshach, and Abednego thrown into the blazing furnace for disobeying orders to worship his golden statue and to serve his gods. When the king peeked through the viewing window, he was surprised to see the men walking around in the middle of the fire—unharmed. The three had faith and trust in God that they would be saved.

Make a "peek box" to retell this story. Use a craft knife or scissors to cut a peephole in one end of the shoebox. Remove the lid and cut a rectangular opening in the top to let in light. Arrange figures and scenery to face the peephole. In addition to the three figures, add a silhouette to represent the mysterious fourth person in the furnace. Figures can be made by the following methods: draw with crayons or markers, then cut out; construct from colored paper; or cut persons and objects from Sunday school leaflets. Characters made using any of these methods should be supported with strips of cardboard to allow the figures to stand up. Bend the strip into an *L* shape, attach the longer portion along the back of each piece, and glue the bent part to the floor of the box. For freestanding forms, shape chenille stems into figures and fashion clothing from scraps of cloth or paper.

To create a furnace atmosphere, glue chunks of coal or rocks painted black to the floor of the box. Make flames from tufts of tissue paper and cellophane. Glue the flames throughout the scene. Cover the peephole and the window in the lid with orange or yellow cellophane to add a fiery glow.

Paint the outside of a shoebox with black or gray paint. Place small strips of duct tape along the open side of the box lid to serve as hinges. Write a title or Scripture reference on a piece of light-colored paper and attach it to the shoebox. Peek into the fiery furnace to observe Shadrach, Meshach, and Abednego.

WEAVING

MATERIALS

construction
  paper
scissors
ruler
pencil
glue
marker
clear, self-
  adhesive paper

METHOD

Create a woven mat as a way to remember the names of the people in a particular Bible story. To use the story of Ruth be sure to include the names *Elimelich, Naomi, Orpah, Mahlon, Ruth, Chilion, Boaz, Obed, Jesse, David,* and *Jesus.*

To construct the mat, fold one twelve- by eighteen-inch piece of construction paper in half to be nine- by twelve-inches. Pencil a margin line one inch from the open edges of the paper, opposite the fold. Cut slits into the folded edge, spacing them one inch apart. Stop cutting at the margin line. Open the paper when the cutting is finished.

Cut strips one inch by twelve inches from two other colors of construction paper. Weave the strips under and over the slits in the twelve- by eighteen-inch paper. Each row alternates. If row one begins under, then row two starts over, and so on until the colored strips are woven across the entire width, forming a mat. Fasten any loose ends with a little glue.

Letter the word *Ruth* around all four edges to form a border. In order to protect the mat, cover it with clear self-adhesive paper.

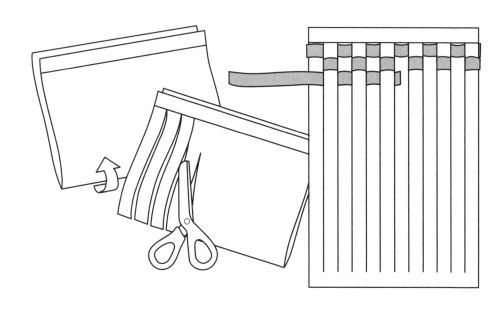

Heart Pattern

Budded Cross Pattern

TELLING THE STORY THROUGH ART: DRAWING AND PAINTING

Art projects offer an excellent way to educate for content; but more importantly, they provide an opportunity to explore and express thoughts and feelings through participation in the process. Ten suggestions for using art, particularly drawing and painting techniques, in teaching and telling biblical stories are provided. The ideas may be combined to develop a lesson or used individually to enhance existing curricula.

DRAWING

EIGHT-FRAME CARTOON

METHOD

As a way to remember a Bible story, draw a series of cartoons to illustrate it. Select a long, narrow strip of paper, 20- by 4-inches, and divide it into six to eight frames. Using drawing instruments, illustrate each scene in a separate square.

Take, for example, the story of Noah and the flood. Write the word Noah in the first square. In each of the folllowing squares, draw: Noah building the Ark (Genesis 6:22); Noah bringing the animals inside (Genesis 7:1); the raging flood (Genesis 7:17); Noah sending out the raven (Genesis 8:7); God making the rainbow as a promise to Noah (Genesis 9:13), and so on.

MATERIALS
Bible(s)
colored pencils
  or fine-tipped
  markers
paper
paper cutter or
  scissors
pencils or pens
rulers

KAMISHIBAI STORY BOX

MATERIALS

Bible(s)
shoebox
calendars,
  catalogs,
  magazines, or
  used Bible story
  leaflets
utility knife
glue
markers
pencils or pens
posterboard or
  heavy paper
scissors

METHOD

Tell the account of the Book—and the life—of Job by making and using a Japanese method of storytelling called a *kamishibai box*, or a *K box*. The front of the box is open to reveal a series of picture cards that have been inserted through a slit in the side. The back of the case is open to allow the narrator to read the words of the story, which are printed on the backs of the cards.

The narrative of the first scene, framed in the open box, is printed on the back of the last card in the series that is at the back of the box. When the narration is completed, the storyteller slides the first card out to display the next scene. The first picture goes to the back of the box to reveal the written story for the scene now in front.

To construct a storytelling box, remove the lid from a shoebox. The opening will be the back of the K box. Using the utility knife, cut out most of the bottom of the shoebox, but leave enough around the edge, approximately one-half inch to make a frame for the pictures. Cut a slit in one side of the box near the cutout opening so that the pictures can easily be inserted or removed. Set the shoebox on its side.

Prepare the story cards. Cut heavy paper or posterboard pieces to a size that will slide in and out of the box but large enough to fit inside the framed front of the box. Select Scripture passages from the story of Job to illustrate. Scenes could provide an overview of his life, or they could highlight one specific portion of the story. An outline to consider might be:

Job loses his wealth, family, and health (1:10–2:13).
Job curses the day of his birth (3:1-26).
The first round of the debate (4:1–14:22).
The second round of the debate (15:1–21:34).
The third round of the debate (22:1–26:14).
Job's closing statements (27:1–30:31).
Job swears that he is innocent (31:1-40).
Elihu's speeches (32:1–37:24).
God's first speech (38:1–39:30).
God's second speech and Job's responses (40:1–42:6).
The Lord again blesses Job with health, wealth, and family (42:7-17).

Draw illustrations or glue pictures from calendars, catalogs, magazines, or used Bible story papers on the individual pages to depict different scenes. Write narrative for each picture, or have the storyteller use his or her own words to interpret the scenes.

Place the cards in the box and use them, one at a time, to share the story of Job.

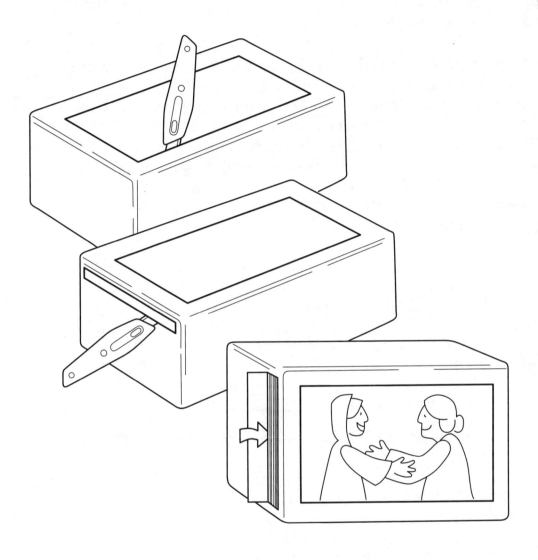

SCROLL

METHOD

The Book of Esther, or Scroll of Esther, is usually referred to as the *Megillah*. The word *Megillah* is the Hebrew word for "scroll," which reminds us that early writings of the Bible were written on rolls of paper. The Megillah is usually written on parchment and sometimes has a wooden winder on one end.

MATERIALS
Bible(s)
colored pencils or
   fine-tip markers
paper: adding
   machine roll,
   mural paper,
   shelf paper, or
   table covering
ribbon
rods: cardboard
   tubes from
   carpet or fabric
   stores or from gift
   wrap, dowels,
   pencils, skewers,
   or toothpicks
scissors

For a small scroll, suitable for individuals to make, cut narrow adding machine tape into a strip approximately twelve inches long. Draw important scenes from the Megillah using colored pencils or fine-tip markers. Glue or tape each end of the strip to a toothpick. Roll the two ends to meet in the middle of the paper strip, or begin at one end and roll the paper all the way to the other end, following the traditional form for the Megillah. Use wider strips of paper and skewers or pencils for another type of small scroll. Tie a ribbon around the rolled paper to finish the scroll.

Larger scrolls, which can be made by groups, can be fashioned in the same way with longer sticks or with long cardboard tubes. Rolls of shelf paper or mural paper work well for drawing and lettering. Use a ruler to mark light pencil guidelines for any words or phrases. Print the captions, along the guidelines, under scenes from the story or between pictures.

Scenes from the Book, and from the life, of Esther to depict include:

King Ahasuerus (Xerxes) has a big party in the palace.
Queen Vashti refuses to attend.
Ahasuerus looks for a replacement for Vashti.
Esther is chosen to be Queen of Persia.
Haman plans to destroy the Jews.
Mordecai discovers Haman's wicked plan.
Mordecai asks for Esther to tell the king the plot.
Esther has dinner with Haman and King Ahasuerus.
Esther tells the king of Haman's plan and that she is Jewish.
Haman is taken away by the guards.
Mordecai is honored by the king.
The Jewish people are saved.
The Feast of Purim is established as a holiday.

Once the project is completed, look over the scrolls to review what happened to Queen Esther.

VIEWER

METHOD

Stories in any book of the Bible—from Genesis through Revelation—bring vivid pictures to mind. Construct a simple viewer to "re-view" one of these accounts.

To construct the viewer, remove the cap and any labels from an empty, clean milk jug. Using scissors, cut a slit on the side of the bottle opposite the handle, about two inches up from the bottom of the jug. The slit will have to be wide enough so the five-inch end of an index card will fit into the container. Place the milk jug aside.

Read the story in the Bible, then decide how to portray the events. Place the five- by seven-inch card vertically on a flat surface. Illustrate the stories, using the bottom two-thirds of the cards. On the top of each card, write a title describing the action.

The entire happening may appear on one card or on several cards to develop the sequence of events. If more than one card is used, be sure to add numbers at the top to keep them in order.

Add captions or Scripture references under the picture. When the work on the cards is finished, slide them into the slot of the milk jug viewer. Hold the viewer with the handle down and the card slot on top. Look through the neck opening to re-view the events.

MATERIALS

Bible(s)
colored pencils or
  fine-tip markers
unlined 5- by
7-inch index cards
plastic milk jugs,
  1-gallon size
scissors
utility knife

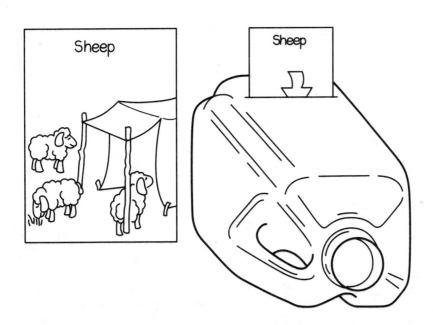

PAINTING

BREATH PAINTING

page 34
Bible(s)
construction
  paper
drinking straws,
  cut in half
food coloring in
  plastic squeeze
  bottles
white paper

METHOD

In Galatians Paul challenges his readers to celebrate the free gift of salvation that God offers to believers. He states that salvation is available through faith in Jesus Christ because of God's grace. Faith in Christ means freedom from the bondage of sin and freedom to love and to serve the risen Savior. The cross of Christ is central to the Christian's celebration of freedom.

Since many celebrations of freedom include a display of fireworks, create a colorful exhibit by using a blow painting technique. Photocopy the breath painting reproducible on page 34.

Using different hues of food coloring as the paint and drinking straws as the paintbrushes, create a fireworks display. Put a drop of food coloring on the photocopy.

Hold a straw perpendicular to the paper, with the end of the straw almost touching the food coloring. Blow through the straw to move the paint and to create interesting designs on the paper. Continue the procedure with additional colors.

When the artwork is dry, mount the picture on a corresponding color of construction paper.

BRICK BOOKENDS

ADVANCE PREPARATION

Clean the bricks and dry them thoroughly.

METHOD

Since Exodus is a book about building, and since bricks are a common building material, construct a set of brick bookends to use as reminders that our lives are built on God's Laws and that our foundation of faith is built on God's faithfulness.

Select two bricks to use for the project. Cover the bricks with a coat of acrylic paint or leave them natural. Paint words and designs on three sides of each brick. (For bookends, the decorations should be painted vertically.) Write the Ten Commandments on the bookends—the first four, emphasizing our relationship with God on one brick, and the last six, focusing on our relationship with others, on the second brick.

Once the designs are completed, cover each brick with acrylic spray, or paint it with several coats of shellac. This part of the process should be done with adult supervision in a well-ventilated place.

Cut felt to fit the bottom of each brick. Glue the felt in place. This will prevent the brick from scratching furniture.

MATERIALS

acrylic paints
Bible(s)
bricks
felt
glue
paintbrushes
scissors
shellac or spray
  acrylic

BUBBLE PRINT

MATERIALS

Bible(s)
drinking straws
food coloring
liquid
  dishwashing
  detergent
mixing bowl(s)
newspaper
white paper
pens
water

METHOD

Combine the fun activity of bubble printing with an opportunity to celebrate the joy of the Christian life. Paul's theme for the Book of Philippians is that real joy results from knowing Jesus and from a life grounded in God.

To start the process, cover a table with newspaper. Pour one-fourth cup liquid dishwashing detergent into a mixing bowl; add a small amount of water and a few drops of food coloring. Practice blowing bubbles through a straw. Don't suck in, or the result will be a mouthful of soap! Blow into the bowl until bubbles rise to the top. Gently lay a sheet of white paper over the bubbles to make a colorful print on the sheet. Once the bubble print is dry, write the letters of the word *Joy* in the circles or shapes.

MARBLE PAINTING

MATERIALS

Bible(s)
boxes (shirt
  boxes work
  well)
containers for
  paint
marbles
paper
spoons
tempera paint,
  five colors

METHOD

As a way to remember facts about a Bible story, participate in a marble painting project. It could be done as an individual activity with each person making his or her own painting or as a group project with each participant using a different color paint to highlight a specific category of information (who, what, when, where, why).

Select a box and put a piece of paper inside of it. Dip a marble in paint; be sure that it is completely covered with the color.

Use a spoon to lift the marble out of the paint and set it on the paper in the box. Tilt the box, letting the marble roll around to create a work of art. State the first category—for example, "Who." Continue the process until several colors and categories have been used. It might be helpful to make a chart to help remember the connection between each color and its category.

Once the painting is dry, this information could be printed along the lines of the picture.

POINTILLISM PICTURE

METHOD

As a way to remember a Bible verse, create a painting using an art technique known as *pointillism*. Pointillism is a French style of painting using dots of color that blend together when viewed from a distance.

Using a pencil, lightly print the chosen words on a piece of paper. Select a pencil to use as a brush and dip the eraser in paint. Make one dot at a time to cover the outline of the words on the sheet. Use a different eraser for each paint color. When the painting is completed, look at the paper from a distance, and notice the way the dots blend to form the words.

MATERIALS
acrylic or
  tempera paint
cleanup supplies
paper
pencils with
  new erasers

SAND PAINTING

METHOD

In the Book of Genesis, God tells Abraham that his descendants will be as numerous as the grains of sand on the seashore. Create a sand painting to picture this promise. Cut a piece of posterboard to the desired size. Use a pencil to letter the key words on the paper.

Cover a work surface with newspaper. Choose an area of the posterboard to be covered with a single color of sand. Spread white glue over the section. Sprinkle the desired color of sand over the glue. Allow the glue to dry. Hold the posterboard over a clean sheet of newspaper. Tap the picture lightly so the loose sand falls onto the newspaper. Use the newspaper to funnel the sand back into the bag or container from which the sand was taken.

Glue another small area and follow the same procedure. Continue until the painting is completed. Display the project as a way to share information about the Book of Genesis.

MATERIALS
Bible(s)
pencils
posterboard
sand, various
  colors
scissors
small bags or
  containers
white glue
newspaper

TELLING THE STORY THROUGH CREATIVE WRITING

Creative writing activities and projects can be used to help children—as well as youth and adults—discover and develop creative, yet concrete, ways to explore biblical stories and themes. It is important to remember to emphasize the expression of ideas and emotions rather than the mastery of mechanics, and to concentrate on content instead of on form.

Creative writing activities should be adapted to the age and abilities of the students. Include younger children in projects by having them dictate their ideas to an older pupil or to an adult, or by providing cassette recorders into which they may speak their sentences and stories. Assistance may be offered in spelling, punctuation, and grammar if a child requests it or if a final editing is necessary.

Ten suggestions for using creative writing in teaching and telling biblical stories are provided. The ideas may be combined to develop a lesson or used individually to enhance existing curricula.

ACCORDION-FOLDED BOOK

ADVANCE PREPARATION

Cut paper lengthwise into strips that are six by eighteen inches.

METHOD

Make an accordion-folded book and fill it with interesting information about the life of a person from the Bible. Take two 6- by 18-inch pieces of white paper and match up two of the short ends. Place the ends together, but do not overlap them. Carefully tape the paper to form a 6- by 36-inch strip. Fan-fold the strip into eight equal sections that will be 4½ by 6 inches. Press the folds for sharp creases. Place the booklet on a table and letter the name of the biblical person, such as David, on the top section. Review Scripture passages in the Books of First and Second Samuel for ideas to add to each page: Samuel annoints David; David becomes king over Israel; David brings the ark to Jerusalem; David receives God's promise for the Messiah; David prepares materials to build the Temple; David instructs his son Solomon about the Temple construction. Using crayon or marker, add illustrations. Tie a ribbon around the completed book.

MATERIALS

Bible(s)
crayons or
    markers
ribbon
rulers
scissors
tape
12- by 18-inch
    white drawing
    paper

CHOOSE-YOUR-OWN-ADVENTURE STORY

METHOD

Writing in response to the story of a person of faith can be a powerful tool for understanding the significance of human choices. Many people should be familiar with a "choose-your-own-adventure" style of writing. In such stories writers pause at critical moments and let readers have a choice in how the plot progresses. If one choice occurs, the resulting story will have one outcome; if the opposite happens, the plot will develop quite differently.

As a biblical story such as the story of Esther unfolds, many characters are faced with decisions that impact the story's outcome. Obviously, the most important choice occurs when Esther decides to go to the king on behalf of her people. Brainstorm critical moments in the story, starting from the beginning when Vashti refuses to go to the king. List as many of these moments as possible. Select one of the critical moments and write an alternative choice and result. Read the stories as a group, or leave the creative writing projects in a place for others to review.

MATERIALS

Bibles or
    children's Bibles
paper
pencils

DICTIONARY/ VOCABULARY WORDS

METHOD

The Bible includes many difficult words that need to be understood by Christians of all ages—those new to the faith, as well as those mature in their beliefs. Create a dictionary—a list of vocabulary words and their explanations—as a way to define, or interpret, some of the terms in the Bible or in a specific book or story. For example, look through Paul's Epistle to the Romans to find key words and unfamiliar terms that need to be explained. Be sure that the selection of words includes concepts such as faith, grace, and saints, as well as terms such as justification, righteousness, and sanctification.

Work individually or in small groups to locate definitions in standard dictionaries and in Bible reference books. Select paper and pencils or pens and create a "dictionary" by listing the selected words in alphabetical order and writing a phrase or a sentence to explain each of them. For example, Faith—complete trust; Grace—undeserved favor from God; and Sin—separation from God. Once the list is compiled, add a decorative cover. Punch the pages and bind them with ribbon, string, or yarn. Share the dictionaries so that others may gain a better understanding of these important words from Romans, as well as grasp the meaning of Gods' great love for each of God's children.

MATERIALS
Bibles
Bible dictionary
dictionary
paper punch
paper
pencils or pens
ribbon, string, or
  yarn
scissors

FLIP BOOK

METHOD

Retell one or more of the stories recorded in the Bible by making and using a flip book. To illustrate the story of the Battle of Jericho, read the account in Joshua 6. Use index cards. Or cut ten small pieces of paper, approximately three by five inches each, and a pencil. On the first piece of paper draw a picture of the walls of the fortified city. On the second page draw the walls starting to collapse; and on pages three through nine illustrate progressive stages of the crumbling of the walls. On page ten draw a pile of rubble on the ground. Color the pictures with pencils, markers, or crayons.

Stack the drawings in order, with page one on the top and page ten on the bottom. If desired, add a front and back cover that may include title, reference, and artist's name. Staple the pages together on the left side of the papers. Flip the book and watch the walls collapse.

MATERIALS
Bible(s)
colored pencils,
  crayons, and/or
  markers
construction
paper or index
  cards, 3 by 5
  inch
pencils
scissors
stapler and staples

LETTER TO GOD

METHOD

God's Word, the Bible, reminds us to put God—the one true God—first in our lives. Look up the Ten Commandments, Exodus 20, in a Bible and read verse 3: "You shall have no other gods before me." Have the children write a letter centering on ways to put God first in life. This letter, to be addressed to God, should contain promises to be kept during a designated period of time, such as a season, month, or year. Examples of promises might be "I promise to spend more time reading the Bible than playing video games," or "I promise to give some of my allowance to help someone else." Be honest and write about topics such as school, family, and friends.

Photocopy page 41 for each child. Encourage each one to compose a letter. When it is completed, address an envelope to each person, put the note inside, and seal the letter with a sticker. Leave the letter for the leader to mail at a future date to review the commitment to keep God first in life.

MATERIALS
page 41
Bibles
envelopes (one
  per person)
pencils
pens
stickers

LITANY

METHOD

A litany is a prayer to God that has one phrase that is repeated after each of the other thoughts. Write an individual litany, or add a phrase to a group prayer, offering praise for the many ways that we can come to God in worship.

Look through copies of the "Order of Worship" in one or several church bulletins. On scrap paper make a list of some of the elements of worship, such as hymns, offerings, prayers, and Scripture readings. Then use these parts of the worship service as a guide for composing the lines. Follow each thought with a phrase such as, "We worship You, O God." Phrases to include in the litany might be:

> When we sing, God, we praise you.
> We worship you, O God.
> When we confess our sins, God, we ask for your forgiveness.
> We worship you, O God.

Use the litany as a personal prayer or share it with the class, family, or friends.

MATERIALS
church bulletins
paper
pencils or pens

NEWSPAPER

METHOD

Look up the word *chronicle* in a dictionary. It is defined as a historical record. A chronicle might be compared to a newspaper since it contains accounts of events. Create a chronicle—a newspaper—to share information about the contents of a book such as First Chronicles. Each participant may prepare one newspaper, or each student could add one story to a group project.

Select a large sheet of paper such as newsprint, 12- by 18-inch construction paper, or 11- by 17-inch copy paper to use as the background of the newspaper. Fold the piece in half. Create the stories and pictures on individual sheets of paper. Use markers, pens, or pencils to write news and to draw illustrations. Cover the facts about First Chronicles by including topics such as: First Chronicles is the thirteenth book of the Bible; it details the reign of David; and it reports that the Messiah will come from the line of David.

After pictures are drawn, stories are written, or activities are completed, arrange the layout in an attractive format and attach the pieces to the newspaper sheet.

MATERIALS

Bible(s)
dictionary
glue sticks
large sheets of
  paper such as
  newsprint,
  construction
  paper, or 11- by
  17-inch copy
  paper
markers, pencils,
  or pens
scissors

SHAPE BOOK

METHOD

Create a shape book to illustrate the meaning of an important biblical passage, such as the Ten Commandments. Photocopy page 42 five times. For younger children, write one commandment, including its number, on each one of the tablets. Photocopy all five pages for each child. For older children, have the Ten Commandments written and displayed so that the children can write them on the tablets. Each child will also need two pieces of colored construction paper for the front and back covers. Using markers and magazine pictures, create an illustration for each commandment on its respective page. Then use words to summarize the meaning of each of God's laws.

Design a front and a back cover for the book. Stack the pages in order and punch two holes on the side of each page. Tie the papers together with ribbon, string, or yarn. Share your ideas with others by leaving the shape book until the end of the session.

MATERIALS

page 42
Bibles
cardboard
construction paper
glue
paper punch
markers
old magazines
pencils
ribbon, string, or
  yarn

STORY STEMS
ADVANCE PREPARATION

MATERIALS
Bibles
chalkboard and
  chalk or
  newsprint and
  marker
paper
pencils

Pre-write the "Story Stems" (see below) on a chalkboard or a piece of newsprint. As an alternative, duplicate a copy for each participant.

METHOD

Use "Story Stems" as the basis of a creative writing project to help each participant acknowledge what Jesus means to him or her. Review the story of Peter's profession of faith, recorded in Matthew 16:16. When Jesus asked the disciples, "Who do you say that I am?" Peter was the first to answer: "You are the Messiah, the Son of the Living God." If we claim that answer, we live with the hope of eternal life that Jesus offers to those who believe in him as their Savior. Refer to the "Story Stems" that have been written on a chalkboard or on a piece of newsprint. They might include:

If you say that Jesus is truly the Christ, the Son of the Living God . . .

  . . . When did you discover the truth that Jesus is your Savior?
  . . . Who helped you acknowledge Jesus' place in your life?
  . . . Can others learn this truth by observing your life of faith?

Provide paper, pencils or pens, and Bibles. Allow time for each person to complete his or her responses. Assure the group that their answers will be kept private if they do not wish to share them with others.

WAX PAPER MESSAGE
METHOD

MATERIALS
Bibles
colored pencils
pens
wax paper
white paper

One of the reasons that the Bible is important is that it helps pass God's truths from one generation to the next. This historical record was intended to remind God's people that because God was at work in the past, God can be trusted to work in the present—and in the future. God was faithful to the people of Israel, and God is faithful to us today. This is still an important message to pass on to others.

Write this message, in a personal way, to share with someone else. For example: God is faithful; Love God with all your heart; Worship God with your life. Place a piece of wax paper over a sheet of white paper. Write the message on the wax paper, pressing down hard, so the wax will transfer to the page. Discard the wax paper. Offer the message to another person. Provide instructions to rub a colored pencil across the page to make the message visible.

Dear God,

_____

_____

_____

_____

_____

_____

_____

_____

_____

_____

_____

Yours truly,

_____

You shall have no other gods before me.
Exodus 20:3

41

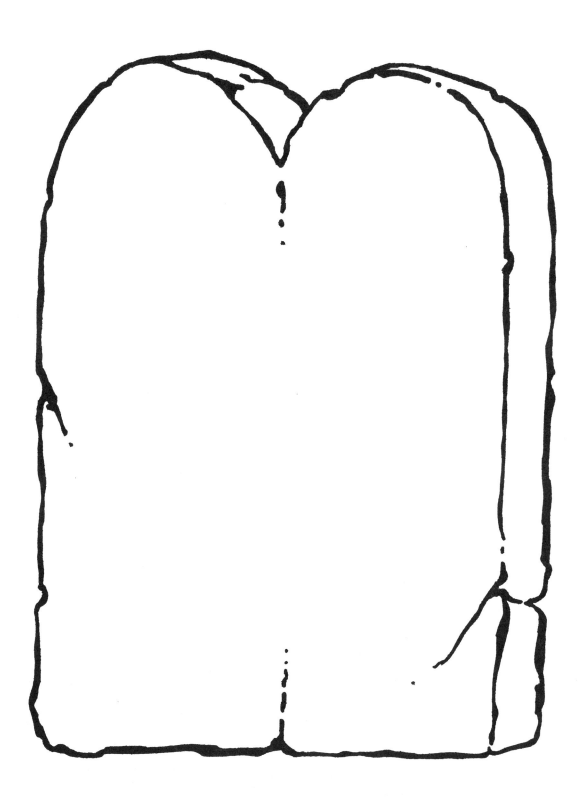

TELLING THE STORY THROUGH CREATIVE WRITING: POETRY

Tell the Bible story through poetry. The variety of styles of poetry make this an attractive method to use with children, as well as with youth and adults. While many people appreciate hearing the compositions of others, they especially enjoy creating their own poems. Poetry can be used as a storytelling method for numerous lessons and in a number of learning situations. Ten ideas and activities to help young people explore biblical and faith themes and concepts through poetry are provided. There are many other poetry formats and formulas to try too.

A-Z POEM

METHOD

Select a subject, such as the attributes of God, and develop an A to Z poem of praise. Begin the poem by printing "God is . . ." on a piece of newsprint. Write the alphabet down the left side of the paper. Then, for every letter, brainstorm adjectives that describe attributes of God. Look through the psalms to discover some of the characteristics and qualities of God; for example: God is forgiving, just, loving, merciful, and powerful. Use a dictionary or a thesaurus to help locate words; for example: A—Awesome, F—Faithful, S—Steadfast, T—Trustworthy, and so forth. Record the ideas on paper. Consider having individuals or small groups brainstorm several letters and compile the poem as a cooperative effort. In addition, offer each child a piece of construction paper and the opportunity to compose his or her own A–Z poem.

MATERIALS
Bible(s)
construction paper
newsprint
dictionary
markers
thesaurus

ACROSTIC POEM

METHOD

Since five diverse books of the Old Testament—Job, Psalms, Proverbs, Ecclesiastes, and Song of Solomon—are known as Poetry, sometimes called Writings, construct an acrostic poem to describe each text. In an acrostic poem, letters of a word are printed vertically down the left side of the page. A word, phrase, or sentence beginning with each letter is then written to develop the topic. For example:

P oetic books in the Old Testament help us
O bserve suffering in the Book of Job;
E xplore prayer and praise in Psalms;
T each tips for successful living in Proverbs;
R espond to the meaning of life in Ecclesiastes;
Y earn for a loving relationship like Christ and the church in Song of Solomon.

Offer paper and pencils or pens and have each student create an acrostic poem on this theme or a topic that connects with a current lesson. Share the results, as each poem will turn out differently.

MATERIALS
Bible(s)
paper
pencils or pens

BIO POEM

ADVANCE PREPARATION

Photocopy a "Growing Christian" bio poem form on page 150 for each student.

Cover a bulletin board with fabric or paper backing material.

METHOD

In 1 Timothy 4:12, Paul reminds his youthful co-worker that there is a place in God's church for people of all ages. In keeping with this theme, create a "Growing Christians" bulletin board. Use it to share information about the children of the church with the adults of the congregation. Bio poetry, a creative writing pattern that provides basic information about a person, is a great way to do this. Although the pattern may be modified to include different categories, one possible format would be:

MATERIALS
page 50
Bible(s)
bulletin board
fabric or paper
  background
material for
  bulletin board
pens
instant-developing
  camera and film
stapler and
  staples
tacks

44

Name	One line
Three adjectives to describe the person	Three lines
Child of	One line
Sibling of	One line
Student at	One line
Likes	Two to five lines
Dreams of	One or two lines
Wants to	One or two lines
Wonders what	One line
Fears	One line
Plans	One line
Hopes	One line
Believes	One or two lines

To begin the project, give each student a copy of page 50 and a pen. Help each child write one or two lines for each category; for example "likes" might include favorite foods and "wants to" may list ambitions in school or sports. If possible, take an instant-developing picture of the person and attach it to the paper. Once the information has been prepared, staple or tack each sheet to a bulletin board. Make the congregation aware of this new way to get acquainted with the "Growing Christians" of the church.

CENTO POEM

METHOD

In light of current events, repeat the message of hope that is offered to God's people by writing it in the form of a cento poem. Cento, a style that dates back to the second century, is a Latin word that means patchwork. The objective in this type of creative writing is to put together lines of poetry, each of which is borrowed from the work of a different author. It can be any number of lines and does not have to rhyme.

Choose a subject, such as hope, as the theme of the poem. Find the word in a Bible reference book called a concordance. Look up several verses related to the topic. Borrow a line, or a phrase, from each passage to construct a cento poem. For example:

> ...Do not be afraid; for see—I am bringing you good news of great
> joy for all the people. (Luke 2:10)
> We wait in hope for the Lord; he is our help and our shield.
> (Psalm 33:20 NIV)

Offer paper and pens or pencils for the project. After everyone has had an opportunity to create a cento poem, share the examples with the class.

MATERIALS
Bible(s)
concordance
paper
pencils or pens

45

CLERIHEW POEM

MATERIALS

markers, pencils,
 or pens
paper

METHOD

A clerihew poem is a quatrain—four lines—based on someone's name. It is designed to offer information about the personality of the person described in the poem. The rhyme scheme is AA, BB, which means that the last words of lines one and two rhyme, and the last words of lines three and four rhyme. Create a clerihew based on the name *Christ* and share information about Paul's New Testament teachings about Jesus. For example:

> Christ Jesus is Lord
> And must be adored.
> He's all that I need
> For salvation—indeed!

After a lesson, emphasize the story by offering each participant a piece of paper and a marker, pencil, or pen. Direct the students to print the word *Christ* in the center of the sheet. They may use freehand skill, pre-cut letters, or stencil shapes to form the outline of the word. Guide the group as they create clerihew poems on this theme.

CLUSTER POEM

MATERIALS

Bible(s)
markers
paper
pencils or pens

METHOD

As a way to acknowledge, or thank, God for God's faithful love, write a cluster poem as a class project. Select a piece of paper and print the phrase "Thank You" in the center of the sheet. Next, brainstorm associations, feelings, ideas, and images that come to mind in response to the words *thank you*. Cluster—or group—them on the sheet. Look over the words and offer a prayer expressing thanks for God's blessings, asking forgiveness for forgetting God's gifts, and praising God for God's faithful love. Be sure to include words and phrases that thank God for Jesus, our Savior, and for the great gift of salvation that restores the relationship between God and God's people.

GIVING POEM

METHOD

After his conversion experience, recorded in Acts 9, Paul gave his life to God. Inspired by the Holy Spirit, Paul was God's messenger of the Good News of the Gospel. In the Book of Second Timothy Paul writes, "I have kept the faith," and he challenges all Christians to keep it too. Share the story of Paul by composing a giving poem. This form of creative writing names a subject that gives an interesting gift. The pattern follows:

Line One—An adjective that describes the subject and a noun that forms the subject;

Line Two—Words that describe something given by the subject;

Line Three—A short phrase that describes who or what is receiving the gift;

Line Four—Two or more words that describe when this happens.

An example, based on the life of Paul, might be:

Apostle Paul
Shares God's love
With everyone
At all times.

Organize the students into partners, and instruct each pair to compose a giving poem about the Apostle Paul. Have them select a piece of paper and a pencil or pen and record their words. Conclude by thanking God for the gift of the life of this great missionary.

LAI VERSE POEM

METHOD

Although the Bible talks about God's judgment, it also offers the message of God's justice. Write a poem using an unusual poetry pattern called lai verse to share this theme with today's world. This creative writing has three stanzas with a total of nine lines, three per verse. The syllable count in each stanza is 5, 5, and 2. Although the usual rhyme scheme is AAB in each stanza, lines one and two of the verses can be unrhymed. For example:

MATERIALS
Bible(s)
paper
pencils or pens

God sends a prophet
To give a warning
Judgment.

God gives forgiveness
To all who repent
Justice.

God sends a Savior
To show God's love
Jesus.

Offer paper and pencils. Encourage each child to write one or more lai verse poems. Have the students read what others have written.

LUNE POEM

METHOD

Help the children remember an important message for today's times—God is our real source of security. Follow a poetry pattern known as lune, which ignores syllables and counts words. It has three lines with the following formula:

MATERIALS
Bible(s)
paper
pens

Line 1—three words
Line 2—five words
Line 3—three words

Select eleven words and write a poem to proclaim the message in a new way. Offer supplies for the project and invite each student to compose one or more lune poems to share with others in the class. For example:

God's in control
Our true security is God
Live in peace.

TERCET AND TRIPLET POEMS

METHOD

Explore the theme of God's grace by composing triplet poems. This type of creative writing is a three-line verse. All three lines may rhyme, AAA; the first and last lines may rhyme, ABA; or the last two lines may rhyme, ABB. If the three lines are unrhymed, ABC, the triplet is called a tercet.

Share the teaching of Paul, especially Titus 2:11, "For the grace of God has appeared, bringing salvation to all," and Titus 3:7, "Having been justified by his grace, we might become heirs according to the hope of eternal life." Explain that Paul is saying that God's grace, through the gift of Jesus, not only saves us from our past sins and offers us eternal life in the future, it also helps us to live a Christian life in the present. Compose a triplet poem on the theme of God's grace; for example:

> God's grace was given just for me;
> God loves me more than I can see;
> I want to share God's love with everyone I meet!

Offer the children paper and pencils or pens, and guide the group as they follow the pattern to create triplet, or tercet, poems.

Bio POEM

(Your name)

_____

(Three adjectives that describe you)

_____, _____, and _____

Child of _____

Sibling of _____

Student at _____

Likes _____

_____

Dreams of _____

_____

Wants to _____

_____

Wonders what _____

Fears _____

Plans _____

Hopes _____

Believes _____

TELLING THE STORY THROUGH CULINARY ARTS

Focusing on food is an enjoyable and educational way to help children explore biblical stories and concepts. The account of the feeding of the five thousand, John 6:1-13, illustrates not only Jesus' use of food as a teaching tool, but also the importance he placed on sharing with and caring for others.

The ten activities suggested are intended to help young people become more aware of the customs and cultures of people around the world. They are also designed to challenge the participants to realize that choosing foods that are good for them and that require less energy to grow, process, and prepare will result in stewardship of the world's limited resources and, therefore, in more food for all people. Biblical themes and topics such as hunger awareness, stewardship of God's gifts, multicultural understanding, and cooperation can be addressed in taste-pleasing and thought-provoking ways through the teaching tool of the culinary arts.

BREAD

METHOD

Ask the children to name a type of food that is part of almost every meal. Bread, in various forms and flavors, is generally served three times a day. It may be toast for breakfast, sandwiches for lunch, and rolls for dinner. Tell the children that for many people of the world, bread is the mainstay of their diet. For some, it may be all they eat in a day. Acquaint the pupils with various types of bread that are commonly used on the seven continents of the world. These may include:

Cornbread from North America
Tortillas, commonly used in South and Central America

MATERIALS
bread, all types
knife
napkins
paper
pens or pencils
scissors

51

Rye, representing Europe
Rice cakes from Asia
Chapatis from Africa
Wheat bread, common in Australia
Marbled bread, depicting people from many continents who live
   and work in Antarctica

Invite the group to sample several selections. Encourage the students to ask their families to use a different type of bread each day for a week as a way to become more aware of people around the world.

Continue the activity by talking with the girls and boys about ways in which bread is used in their own families. Brainstorm how this taken-for-granted staple could be used more sparingly. These ideas may include buying bread at a surplus store, finding out what grocery stores and bakeries do with day-old bread, or using stale bread for crumbs or croutons rather than throwing it away.

Pass out paper that has been cut into the shape of a slice of bread. Provide pens or markers and ask each child to write or draw a way in which he or she will commit to using this resource more carefully and creatively.

CALORIES

ADVANCE PREPARATION
Cut paper for body tracings.

Find calorie statistics for various countries.

MATERIALS
calorie charts
markers
newsprint or
   mural paper
scissors
statistics
tape

METHOD
Living more simply so others may simply live is more than just a phrase. It is an individual choice. Engage the class in an activity that will help them compare the food they eat and the total number of calories they consume to what is available to people in other parts of the world. In advance, obtain statistics from a denominational or world hunger relief organization on the number of calories people in various parts of the world consume per day. This is also available from Internet sites and the reference section of a library. Resources state that a person needs approximately 2,350 calories per day. In the United States the average per-person daily calorie intake is 3,665. In Mozambique it is 1,632. Make a poster or chart containing this information and hang it in the room. Also exhibit calorie charts.

Pair the students and have each person make a life-size body tracing on newsprint or mural paper. It would be helpful to have lengths of paper cut in advance. Pass out two pieces to each set of partners. Instruct the children to place the paper on the floor, to have one person lie down on a piece, and to have the other person use a marker to trace his or her partner's outline onto the sheet. When the first drawing is completed, have the pupils switch roles and make the second drawing. As the children finish, tell them to cut out their tracings.

Provide markers and ask the students to draw their faces, as well as any other simple decorations, on the figures. Tell the children to draw pictures on the papers of everything they have eaten in the last day. This includes meals as well as snacks. Hand out pieces of tape and have the learners hang the pictures in the room.

Show the children how to use the calorie charts to calculate the total number of calories they might have consumed the day before. Demonstrate how to compare these figures to the intake in various countries.

Discuss ways in which the children may eat more simply and more sensibly and how this can contribute to food for others.

COMMUNITY PROJECT
ADVANCE PREPARATION
Research community projects to which food may be donated.

METHOD
There are many needs and opportunities for sharing food in a community. These could include soup kitchens, homeless shelters, missions, prisons, group homes, and extended care facilities. Enable the children to become aware of some of these through the use of speakers, audio-visual materials, newspaper articles, and field trips.

As a group, choose a project and get involved. Some ideas would be to bake bread and bring it to an institution, to prepare and package muffins and share them with other people, or to make soup and serve it at the selected site. Use favorite recipes or recipes from books at the library or from sources on the Internet.

Emphasize to the students that giving and sharing are two important actions of followers of Jesus. Food ministries are only one way to demonstrate these important qualities.

MATERIALS
cooking
  equipment and
  utensils
ingredients
recipe(s)
resource
  materials

COOPERATIVE MEAL

METHOD

MATERIALS
cooking and
  serving
  equipment
ingredients for
  recipe

Cooperation is essential in a classroom. It is also a key ingredient in many Bible stories such as Jesus and the disciples ministering throughout Galilee, and Paul and the disciples teaching in Asia and Europe. To illustrate this point, invite the children to share a special lunch or snack to which everyone contributes an item and cooperates in the planning and preparation process.

Discuss some meals that could be made in this manner.

These might be tacos where the shells—tortillas—are provided, and cheese, lettuce, and tomato are purchased; rice with a variety of items such as chicken, celery, pineapple, and coconut to put on top; fruit salad for which each person brings one ingredient; broth or stock combined with various vegetables to make soup; pancakes or waffles with unusual toppings; or bread with several selections of spreads and condiments.

In advance, assign each participant a specific item to bring for the meal. Prepare or purchase the base, such as bread or rice. Include preparation time as part of the process. Guide the children as they combine the ingredients to be used.

As the meal is shared, talk about ways in which the contributions and cooperation of many people could help eliminate world hunger.

INGREDIENTS

METHOD

MATERIALS
baking
  equipment
coated chocolate
  candies
ingredients for
  cookie dough
recipe

During a study of the last Beatitude found in Matthew 5:10, "Blessed are those who are persecuted for righteousness' sake, for theirs is the kingdom of heaven," use a mixer to blend ingredients to make cookie dough. Discuss how each ingredient "disappears" as the dough comes together. Explain that as Christians we need to be in the world, but not of the world. We need to remain faithful and distinct even though the going gets tough.

Add an ingredient such as coated chocolate candies to the cookie dough and stir. Point out that, like Christians, the candies hold their identity even as they are blended into the mix. Bake the cookies and enjoy.

PACKAGING

ADVANCE PREPARATION

Create a display of food-packaging materials.

Place the appetizing snack in an unappealing container and put the unappetizing snack in an appealing container.

METHOD

Unfortunately, people are often judged by the way they look on the outside rather than by who they are on the inside. Illustrate this point by using packaging materials from a variety of food products. Wrappers and advertising may make food seem appealing, but the products might not taste as good as they appear. Emphasize this fact by offering the children a snack. Show the group two boxes and tell them that they must agree on the one from which they want their treat. One box should be extremely attractive, enticingly labeled, and beautifully decorated. The other container should be extraordinarily unappealing in its outward appearance. Ask the group to choose one box, gently encouraging them to pick the most attractive one. Open the box and show the children an unappealing snack. Open the other box and show the group a treat they would all like. Set both boxes aside.

Invite the participants to look closely at the display of food-packaging materials. Challenge the group to think about a variety of questions. What do the labels tell? What don't they tell? Are they misleading in any way? Are some labels unattractive? Does unattractive mean what's inside isn't good? Do people try the product if it doesn't look good? Might the product be good even if the packaging is unattractive? Provide paper and pens and encourage the students to record their responses. Ask if these questions also relate to people. How might people be different on the inside and the outside? Isn't it much like the labels of food?

Invite the children to compile a list of the "ingredients" that make them special. Emphasize that the list should include things that people can't tell just by looking at them. For example: artist, poet, cook, kind, loving, compassionate, lonely, sad. Ask those who are willing to share some of their responses.

Once again, display the unappealing box containing the appealing snack. Ask the children if they would like to share the treat together, even though on the outside it doesn't look like something they would enjoy. Continue the discussion while eating together.

MATERIALS
boxes, two
labels and
   wrappers from
   food products
paper
pencils or pens
snacks, one
   appetizing and
   one unappetizing

PRETZELS

MATERIALS
1¼ cups warm
  water (105–115
  degrees F)
1 package active
  dry yeast
½ teaspoon sugar
4½ cups sifted
  flour
1 egg yolk
1½ tablespoon
  milk
coarse salt
mixing and
  baking
  equipment
towel
optional:
  refrigerated
  bread dough

METHOD

Pretzels were made by Roman monks in the fifth century and distributed to the poor on certain days before Easter. Because the dough, often made from only flour, salt, and water, was twisted to represent two arms crossed in prayer, pretzels were symbols that reminded the people of the holiness of the season.

Prepare pretzels in advance, or use the activity as a class project. To make the pretzels, dissolve the yeast and sugar in the warm water. Allow it to stand one hour. Mix in the flour. Knead the dough for seven or eight minutes. Place the dough in a greased bowl. Cover it with a towel and let it rise until it is doubled in size. Form the dough into pretzels. Place the pretzels on a greased cookie sheet. Mix the egg yolk and milk together, and brush it over each pretzel. Sprinkle generously with coarse salt. Allow the pretzels to rise until not quite double in size. Bake in a preheated oven at 475 degrees for about ten minutes. This recipe will yield eleven six-inch pretzels.

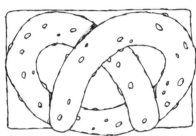

For an alternative recipe, use refrigerated bread stick dough to form the pretzels. Shape the dough into pretzels. Brush each piece with the egg yolk and milk mixture and sprinkle them with the salt. Bake according to the package directions.

SMORGASBORD

MATERIALS
cookbooks
equipment
ingredients
information on
  festivals

METHOD

Tasting the cuisine of various countries may encourage an appreciation for and an understanding of the people who live there. Ask the children to think about people in the congregation and the community and to name some of their countries of origin. In advance, obtain information on ethnic neighborhoods or festivals in the area to share with the group.

Hold an international smorgasbord and allow the students to taste the foods from various places. Center the menu on the dishes of one country; or for more variety, serve samples of items from all over the world. If the learners are to be involved in the preparation, find a cookbook for children that includes easy ethnic dishes.

Invite guests from the countries represented by the foods to share the meal, as well as to bring information that may help the youngsters gain insight on those nations and their peoples.

SYMBOL

ADVANCE PREPARATION
Make a "peace" words poster below. Prepare cupcakes and frostings.

METHOD
An Irish custom involving cupcakes can be used to help children recognize and appreciate a worldwide need for peace. It can also encourage a positive concept of peace all over the earth.

Begin by showing the young people pictures of people, especially children, from various countries. Ask them to guess where they might live. Provide a globe or world map and help the learners locate some of these places on it. Discuss ways in which these children also want peace.

Explain an Irish custom of giving a cupcake to someone with whom you would like to make peace. On a piece of posterboard, write the word *peace* in several languages.

Some words to include are:

French—Paix
German—Frieden
Hungarian—Beke
Irish—Slochain
Italian—Pace
Polish—Pokoj
Russian—Mir
Spanish—Paz
Swahili—Usalama
Swedish—Fred

Guide each pupil in choosing a word to use in a special activity.

Surprise the children with undecorated cupcakes and several colors of frosting. Give each person a cupcake and assist him or her in writing *peace* on it in the language selected. Invite the group to give the cupcakes to someone as an offering of peace. Better yet, have each student make two: one to eat and one to share.

cupcakes, undecorated
frosting, various colors
globe or world map
knives
marker
napkins
pictures
posterboard

WORLD RELIGIONS

food items
information on
special occasions
in other cultures

METHOD

The culinary arts may be used to introduce children to several major world religions, since food is often a focal and festive part of the commemoration of religious holidays. This would be an interesting way to highlight the topic of various faith traditions. Bring information and food items related to the specific occasion, such as:

Christianity: On Easter, Christians often have large dinners that include lamb, representing Jesus the Lamb of God, and boiled eggs, symbolizing new life.

Judaism: Passover meals involve unleavened bread and other foods that are used to retell the story of the Israelites' deliverance from Egypt.

Hindi: In celebration of the Hindu New Year, which falls in April or May, people go to the temples for prayer and then return home for elaborate feasts and gift exchanges.

Buddhism: During a three-day festival that reminds people of the life of Buddha, everyone goes to the temple to listen to the holy scriptures. In the evening they light candles, eat, and celebrate together.

Baha'is: On the first day of spring, which is also the first day of their new year, Baha'is break a fast with special prayers and potluck dinners.

Islam: Mohammed's birthday is commemorated with nine days of fairs and parades. Favorite foods are tabouleh—wheat, mint, onions, and tomatoes—and roast chicken filled with rice, spices, and ground lamb.

TELLING THE STORY THROUGH GAMES: GAME FORMATS

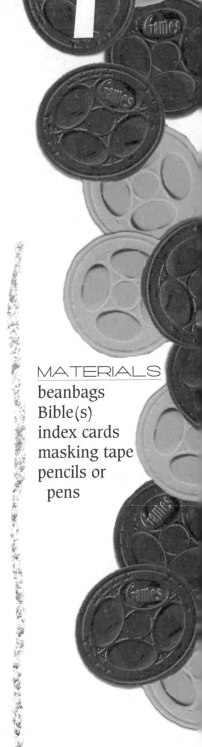

People of all ages and abilities, and with no prior experience, can enjoy and learn from games. Games are a great way to mix people, and in the process, strengthen relationships. When children work together, instead of against one another, the elements of advantage and the fear of being eliminated are removed.

Ten popular or traditional game formats are suggested as tools for teaching biblical stories and scriptural themes. They do not require expensive equipment or time-consuming preparation. Try any or all of these ideas to teach lessons in interactive ways.

BEANBAG TOSS

ADVANCE PREPARATION

Number sets of index cards from one to twenty. Set one batch of cards aside to distribute to the participants. Tape the other set to the floor to form a game board for the beanbag toss activity. One possible pattern would be to create four rows, with five cards in each row. Be sure to leave several inches of space between each card.

METHOD

In the New Testament Paul emphasizes Christian love. He stresses the responsibility of every Christian to use the gifts God has given us in: service to God and others; ways to spread the Gospel and reach out to those in need; helping to build the church, which is the body of Christ. Invite each participant to think about ways to do these things.

MATERIALS
beanbags
Bible(s)
index cards
masking tape
pencils or
    pens

59

Distribute one or more numbered index cards and pencils or pens to each person and instruct everyone to write an idea on the back of each paper. For example, you could suggest: bring a friend to Sunday school, invite a neighbor to a worship service, help at a church cleanup day, read a Bible story to someone who is ill and unable to leave home, and volunteer for a mission agency. Collect the cards.

To play the game, one person tosses a beanbag into one of the squares. He or she then reads the statement on the index card with the same number. Invite the rest of the group to respond to the declaration with words of affirmation such as "I'll do that too," "Let's try it," or "Yes." To vary the activity, participants may play the game as individuals or as teams. Players may select a square and try to throw a beanbag on it, or they may toss at random.

CHECKERS

METHOD

MATERIALS
Bible(s)
board for
  checkers game
checkers
index cards
pencils or pens

Play a game of checkers to review information about a Bible story. After reading or telling the story, prepare ten to twenty questions about it on separate index cards. When the cards are completed, set the checkerboard on a table or on the floor. Place a checker for each player on a square at the bottom of the board. Shuffle the cards and put them in the center of the game. In turn, players draw a card, read the question, and attempt to answer it.

If the answer is correct, the player may move a marker up one square. If it is incorrect, the player moves it back one space—maybe even off the board. Continue drawing cards and moving markers until one person reaches the top of his or her row. Follow this plan at least three times. Remember that regardless of who reaches the top of the board first, everyone wins when he or she learns more about God's Word.

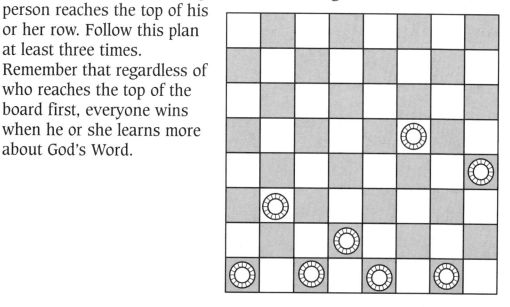

BLINDMAN'S BLUFF TAG

METHOD

The Gospel of Mark is a book of action that records Jesus' miracles and parables. Since the Book of Mark contains the story of Jesus healing the blind, try a version of "Blindman's Bluff," a game of tag, to learn the events of the story. One player, the blindman, is blindfolded. Everyone else joins hands and walks in a circle around the blindman. When the blindman claps three times, the circle stops. The blindman points and asks a player to answer a question about the story. If the player responds correctly, the blindman remains blindfolded. If the player responds incorrectly, the blindman and the player exchange places. Continue the game in this manner until several players have been the blindman.

MATERIALS
Bible(s)
blindfold

DOMINOES

METHOD

Create a game of dominoes and use it to review "Who, What, When, Where, and Why" information about a Bible story. Begin by lettering the five *W* words on a sheet of paper, leaving space between each one. Look through the Bible story and record information for each category. Use this information to create a game of dominoes. For a two-player game, select nine index cards, and cut each of them in half lengthwise. Draw a line down the center of each cut card. Then, on either side of the line, print one of the "Five W" words. Each word should be used three times. Vary the combination of words on the dominoes.

To play the game, place the dominoes face down and mix them up. Each player draws five dominoes. The player selected to go first places any domino face up between the two players. The second player then plays a domino that matches the word on either end. If that player does not have a matching domino, he or she draws from the unused pile. The player keeps drawing until a matching domino is found, or until they are all gone. In that case the play passes back to the first player. In any case, the player who matches the words must share information related to that category. For example, if the word *who* is matched, the player must name someone mentioned in the story.

Dominoes may be played end to end or at right angles to the ones already played. The only place to add a domino is at either open end. Play continues until one of the players wins by using up all of his or her dominoes.

MATERIALS
Bible(s)
index cards
paper
pencils or pens
scissors
optional: rulers

DUCK, DUCK, GOOSE

METHOD

God's love has often been compared to a circle, a shape that has no beginning and no end. And the good news is that there's always a place in the circle for us! Emphasize this theme, or review any Bible story, by using an activity involving a circle. Adapt the game "Duck, Duck, Goose" to this format. Review the rules. One player is "It."

Everyone except 'It' sits in a circle. 'It' walks around the outside of the circle, behind the players' backs. 'It' gently taps the players' heads and says, "God," and "Loves." But on one player's head, 'It' taps, says "You!" and starts to run. The person labeled "You" jumps up and chases 'It' around the circle.

If 'You' doesn't tag 'It' before 'It' reaches the vacant spot, 'It' takes the runner's seat. 'You' becomes the new 'It' and must give an example of God's love for him or her. If 'You' does tag 'It', he or she gets back in the circle, and 'It' is 'It' again. Continue play so that several children can be "It."

HOPSCOTCH

MATERIALS
beanbags or
    stones
Bible(s)
materials to form
    hopscotch game:
    carpet squares,
    chalk, or
    masking tape

ADVANCE PREPARATION

Make a hopscotch game to use for the activity. If the game can be played outside, draw a traditional hopscotch game in the dirt or in chalk on the sidewalk. If it is to be played indoors, lay one out with carpet squares. Use masking tape to make a number on each square. If carpet squares aren't available, use masking tape to make both squares and numbers.

METHOD

God gave the Ten Commandments as a guide for life. Sometimes the Ten Commandments are called "rules." In order for the Ten Commandments to be used as rules for living, we must do more than just learn the laws—we must understand what they mean for everyday situations. Play a game of "Commandments Hopscotch." Every game has rules— the established procedures for playing the activity. Follow the rules and use the activity as an opportunity to help the participants relate the commandments to their own lives.

Use the hopscotch game outside or inside, and select a marker such as a stone or beanbag. Throw the marker into one of the numbered squares. Remember to hop on one foot in the single squares, land on both feet in the double squares, and hop over the squares that hold the marker. When someone lands on a block, the person must summarize the commandment that goes with the number in the square. For example, 8—I will be honest on a test; or 10—I will not blame my brother for something that I did. Have the player continue the game until he or she has hopped to the top of the board and back to the beginning.

MIX & MATCH
METHOD

MATERIALS
pages 76–79
Bible(s)
markers
posterboard
yardstick

In any book, including the Bible, the table of contents lists the arrangement of the subject matter. In a Bible, the table of contents lists the books of the Old and New Testaments in sequence and provides page numbers to help the reader locate them. Usually the name of each book is "spelled out" in the table of contents, but often it is abbreviated in other places. It's important to know both ways of locating a book. Use a game of Bible Mix & Match to match the full name of a book with its shortened version.

To make a game board, divide a piece of posterboard into sixty-six equal sections—for example, eleven rows of six. Letter the abbreviation of each book of the Bible, in sequence, in a separate section. Place the game board on a flat surface, such as a table or a desk. Photocopy and cut apart the Bible cards on pages 76–79. (Omit the last column on page 79.)

To play the game, shuffle the cards and stack them in a pile. Participants take turns drawing a card and matching the name to the abbreviation on the board. If a match is made, the card should be placed in the proper section on the board. Use Bibles to check answers. Depending on time, instruct each player to make five or ten matches, or to play the entire game.

OBSTACLE COURSE

MATERIALS

bandannas or
  scarfs
Bible(s)
plastic cones, or
  chairs and tables

METHOD

Jesus, as well as the Old Testament prophets and the New Testament apostles, tells God's people that there will be many false teachers who try to lead them away from listening to God's voice and from following Jesus' example. Sometimes these people even say that Christ's life, death, and resurrection is not important. The teachings of the Bible advise believers against misdirection—going away from God. Even in the midst of changing times, the unchanging truth of the Gospel will help God's people stay on course.

To illustrate this point, play a game involving a cone course—a type of obstacle course—that will show the participants how easy it is to be led astray. Set up a route by using plastic cones to form a challenging path through the playing area. If large cones such as those used in construction zones are not available, use chairs and tables to form the obstacle route.

To play the game, direct the player's attention to the cone course and explain the guidelines for the activity. Organize the participants into three groups. Explain that Group One will try to go through the course blindfolded. Group Two will shout helpful directions, but Group Three will call out false guidance. Then give each person in Group One a bandanna, and help these learners tie the blindfolds around their heads. Tell the members of Group One to join hands or to link arms. Instruct Groups Two and Three to scatter around the course and to begin shouting instructions to direct—or misdirect—Group One through the route. Instruct Group One to attempt to walk from the beginning to the end of the course. After Group One completes the path, have the participants trade roles and play again.

When each group has had a turn to attempt the cone course, ask the players to form a circle and to sit on chairs or on the floor to review the activity. Discuss questions such as: "What made it difficult to go through the cones?" and "What made it easy to move around the course?"

Find a volunteer to locate 2 Peter 3:17-18 in a Bible and to read it to the group. Invite each person to turn to the learner on his or her right. Ask each pair to think of ways that "other voices" try to lead them away from the "voice of God" and from following Jesus' example for our lives. Ideas might include: a classmate says that "everyone else is doing it," a friend remarks "no one will find out," or a movie or television program makes something that is wrong seem right. Ask the partners to discuss ways to be guided by God's voice. Talk about Peter's advice to grow in faith and in the knowledge of Jesus Christ. That could mean reading the Bible to learn how to follow Jesus, talking with a trusted adult about peer pressure, and praying to God for help in a difficult situation.

Conclude the activity by reminding the participants that just as they listened for the right instructions—or voices—in the game, it is important to listen for God's voice as they encounter the obstacles of life.

RED LIGHT, GREEN LIGHT

METHOD

MATERIALS
Bible(s)

"Red Light, Green Light" is not only the name of a popular children's game, but it is also a good way to describe the content of the teachings of the Bible. In Peter's letters to the early churches, he cautions Christians to "Stop" believing false teachers and to "Go" to God's Word to increase their faith in Christ, as well as their knowledge of Jesus' instructions for living a holy life.

After highlighting the basics of Peter's teachings, gather the participants in a large open area and explain the connection, as well as the instructions, for a game of "Red Light, Green Light." Designate one player as the "Traffic Light" and position "It" at one end of the space. Direct the remaining participants to form a line at the other end of the room. Play begins when the "Traffic Light" turns his or her back to the others and says "Green Light." This is a cue for the others to advance toward the light and, ultimately, to try to tag it. At any time the light may say "Red Light" and turn around. "Red Light" is a signal for players to "freeze" in place. Those in motion when the light turns around must return to the starting line, and each one must share a fact about the Book of Second Peter. On the first round, the fact should relate to "Who," the second round to "What," the third to "When," the fourth to "Where," and the fifth to "Why."

Play resumes as the "Traffic Light" alternates calling green and red. Once another player succeeds in touching the "Traffic Light" without being seen, that person becomes the new light.

At the conclusion of the game, remind the players that the message of the Book of Second Peter challenges Christians to "Go" to God's Word to learn the truth about Jesus so that they may "Stop" false beliefs about God's plan of salvation.

TWISTER
METHOD

"Twister" game, or components to create a game, such as construction paper, masking tape, paper plates, or posterboard, scissors, and spinner

In his second Epistle, Peter warns Christians in the New Testament church—as well as Jesus' followers in congregations today— to beware of "false teachers" who twist the truth of God's Word, the Bible. Peter also states that believers—then and now—increase their faith as they grow in their knowledge of Jesus Christ. God's people must study the Scripture in order to learn the truth for themselves. As a way to remember this important message, play a game of "Twister."

Set up a "Twister" game, or prepare a homemade version by creating rows of blue, green, red, and yellow circles on the floor of the playing area. Large circles may be cut from construction paper or posterboard, but colored paper or plastic plates would also work for the project. Form "inside-out" circles of masking tape, place a roll on the bottom of each colored disk, and attach it to the floor. Also prepare a spinner by dividing a circle or a square into four quadrants. In the upper left corner, print "Left Foot," the lower left, "Left Hand," the upper right, "Right Hand," and the lower right, "Right Foot." Use a marker or sticker to place a blue, green, red, and yellow dot in each quarter of the spinner.

To play the game, the first person turns the spinner. The player must then place his or her hand or foot on a colored dot on the game board that corresponds with the color of the circle to which the arrow points and the quadrant in which it lands. Once in position, the person must answer a question about the story. When all players are on the game board, designate someone to turn the spinner and to check for accuracy of answers. Continue the game until all questions have been answered or until the hands and feet of all players have become so twisted that it is impossible to continue the activity.

At the conclusion of the game, remind the participants that there are people who try to "twist" God's Word—people who tell them that believing in Jesus as their Savior is not important and that living a life of faithfulness to God is not necessary. Challenge each person to continue to read the Bible during personal and family devotions, to study God's Word in Sunday school classes and mid-week programs, and to have friends who put Scripture first in their lives.

8

TELLING THE STORY THROUGH GAMES: SEQUENCING GAMES

Since sequencing games are a great method to use to teach biblical stories and scriptural themes, ten techniques are offered as springboard suggestion to use in a variety of children's programs at church. They do not require expensive equipment or time-consuming preparation. Use any or all of these ideas to teach lessons or to tell stories in interactive ways.

BALLOON GAME

ADVANCE PREPARATION

Photocopy and cut apart the Bible slips on pages 76–79. (Omit the last column on page 79.) Roll each slip of paper and place it inside a balloon. Blow up the balloons and tie them shut. Place the balloons in a basket or box or tape them to a bulletin board or a wall. Cut a sheet of posterboard in half. Label one half "Old Testament" and the other half "New Testament," or use appropriate categories. Hang the two signs near the balloons. Place rolls of tape near each sign.

METHOD

Learn the order, or sequence, of the sixty-six books of the Bible—or the thirty-nine books of the Old Testament, the twenty-seven books of the New Testament, or the books of a specific category—by playing a game.

MATERIALS
pages 76–79
balloons
Bible(s)
clear and
  masking tape
basket or box

To play the game alone, select a balloon from the box or the display, pop it, and remove the slip of paper. Read the name of the book of the Bible and decide if it is found in the Old Testament or the New Testament. Tape the name to the correct poster. Pop another balloon and repeat the process. Try to place the papers in sequence—in the order the books appear in the Bible. Other students will take turns and add to the posters. Check the results at the end of the session.

To play the game with another person, take turns popping balloons and putting the names of the books on the posters.

To play the game as a group, or as teams, mark a starting line on the floor with masking tape. Place the container or display of balloons at the opposite end of the room. Line up behind the tape. One player at a time runs to the box, picks a balloon, pops it, and reads the Bible book name printed on the paper. The player runs to the correct poster—Old Testament or New Testament—and attaches the paper to the sign. When the student returns to the end of the line, the next player repeats the procedure. The game continues until all of the books of the Bible are in order on the posters.

CLOTHESLINE SORTING GAME

ADVANCE PREPARATION

String clothesline between two classroom chairs.

METHOD

Review the order, or sequence, of the events of a Bible story by playing a clothesline sorting game. Print a word or a phrase about each part of the narrative on a separate piece of construction paper. Turn the sheets face down, mix them up, and gather them into a stack. In turn, each player picks a paper from the top of the pile, reads the words, and hangs it on the clothesline in its proper sequence. Once the pieces are hung, compare the sequence to the actual events of the Bible story.

Instead of a clothesline, the sheets may be sorted into many other materials, such as cans labeled first, second, and so forth, or manila envelopes designated beginning, middle, and end. For a sequencing activity based on a theme such as the books of the Bible, the names may be written on cups, footprints, or stones, and placed in order.

CLOTHESPIN GAME BOARD

ADVANCE PREPARATION

Photocopy the game board on page 80. Make game pieces out of clothespins.

METHOD

Twenty-one letters, called epistles, form the majority of the New Testament books of the Bible. Thirteen letters composed by Paul are known to be the earliest writings in the New Testament. Called the Pauline Epistles, this correspondence is directed to specific churches and individuals. The last eight epistles are designated as "General" because they are not addressed to specific places or people. Seven of the General Epistles are named for their authors—one each for James and Jude, two for Peter, and three for John. Most scholars consider the authorship of Hebrews to be unknown.

Although each of the letters has its own specific purpose and theme, all twenty-one epistles amplify and clarify the content of the Gospels, stress the importance of correct doctrine, and relate doctrine to daily life.

Play a game to learn the names and the sequence of the New Testament epistles. Photocopy page 80.

To make the playing pieces, count out twenty-two clip clothespins. Using a permanent marker, print the words *New Testament* on one clothespin, and letter the name of each epistle on the remaining twenty-one. If it is not possible to write directly on the plastic or wood, print the words on small pieces of paper and glue or tape them to the clothespins.

Try the game. Mix up the clothespins and place them in a basket or box. Pick one clothespin at a time and read the name of the book that's written on it. First decide if the book is a Pauline Epistle or a General Epistle. Then clip the pin to a square on the board, putting the books in their proper New Testament sequence. The "New Testament" clothespin should be attached to the square labeled "Epistles."

Pauline Epistles: Romans, 1 and 2 Corinthians, Galatians, Ephesians, Philippians, Colossians, 1 and 2 Thessalonians, 1 and 2 Timothy, Titus, and Philemon

General Epistles: Hebrews, James, 1 and 2 Peter, 1, 2, and 3 John, and Jude

MATERIALS
page 80
baskets or boxes
Bibles
clip clothespins,
 22 per game
permanent
 markers

DECK OF BIBLE BOOK CARDS

METHOD

MATERIALS
pages 76–79
Bible(s)
index cards
glue

Make a deck of "Bible Book" cards and use them to play a game to review the order, or sequence, in which the sixty-six books are contained in the Bible. To make a set, photocopy and cut apart pages 76–79. (Omit the last column on page 79.) Glue each name to a separate 3-inch by 5-inch index card. Shuffle the pieces and deal out the entire deck to the players. Each player keeps the cards face down in a pile.

To start, one person turns the top card face up. The player reads the word on the card and must name the book of the Bible that comes before or after it. For example, if the card contained the word "Joel," the player would say that "Hosea" came before "Joel" or that "Amos" came after it. If the word on the card were "Acts," the player would name "John" or "Romans." If the first player cannot answer the question, the second player has an opportunity to try. If the answer is correct, the second player keeps the card. If both players answer incorrectly, they look up the answer in the table of contents of the Bible, and the card is placed in the center of the table.

Play continues until someone runs out of cards. At the end of the game, the players should work together to sequence, or put the cards in the order in which the books are organized in the Bible.

As an additional activity, turn the cards face down, mix them up, and gather them into a stack. In turn, each player picks a card from the top of the pile. If the word on the card is *Genesis*, the name of the first book of the Bible, the player lays the card face up on the table. If it is not *Genesis*, the card is placed face down on the bottom of the pile. Once the *Genesis* card is found, players must continue picking cards until the next book of the Bible is located and placed on the table. Play continues until all cards have been used and the books of the Bible have been placed in sequence.

GIFT WRAP GAME

ADVANCE PREPARATION

To create gift tags, photocopy and cut apart the names of the books of the Bible on pages 76–79. You will not need the two cards labeled "Old Testament" and "New Testament" on page 79.

Include the tag with the words "We learn God's faithfulness in the Book of _____." Cover the Bible with tissue or wrapping paper. Attach the tag for the last book, "Revelation," to the top of the package.

Repeat the process until the Bible is covered in sixty-six layers of paper—one to represent each book of the Old Testament and the New Testament. Attach the correct "label" to each layer—Revelation at the bottom and Genesis on the top. Then wrap the Bible in another layer of paper and add the tag "We learn God's faithfulness in the Book of _____."

As an additional learning device, wrap each category of books, such as Law or History, in the same type or color of paper. Place an additional tag on the first book of each classification.

METHOD

Each of the thirty-nine books of the Old Testament and the twenty-seven books of the New Testament add a layer of learning to our understanding of God's faithfulness—to people long ago and to us today. As a unique activity, unwrap a gift sixty-seven times and review the names of the books of the Bible—the place where we learn about God's love.

Although the game may be played alone, it would be more fun to find a partner or a group of students to share the experience.

Review the names of the books of the Bible by removing layers of paper from the package. The object of the game is to name the books of the Bible in sequence. For example, the first player would name the first book of the Bible, "Genesis," remove one layer of paper, and read the tag to indicate the answer. Everyone is then invited to repeat the phase, "We learn about God's faithfulness in the Book of Genesis." The next player must name the next book of the Bible, "Exodus," remove one layer of paper, read the tag, and invite the group to repeat the phrase. Play continues until the layers of paper have been removed and the Bible is revealed.

MATERIALS
pages 76–79
Bible(s)
tape
tissue or
  wrapping paper
scissors

MAGNETIC SEQUENCING GAME

MATERIALS
pages 77–78
Bible(s)
cookie sheet or
   metal tray
envelopes
magnetic cards
scissors

METHOD

Although they may be called "Major" and "Minor," the seventeen books that form the last section of the Old Testament are all categorized by the word *Prophets*. Major and Minor refer to the length of the books—long or short—not to their importance.

The five major books of the Prophets include Isaiah, Jeremiah, Lamentations, Ezekiel, and Daniel. Minor prophets are Hosea, Joel, Amos, Obadiah, Jonah, Micah, Nahum, Habakkuk, Zephaniah, Haggai, Zechariah, and Malachi.

Try a magnetic sequencing game as an aid to memorizing the names of these seventeen books of the Prophets. Photocopy and cut apart the Prophets cards. Cut a section of magnet long enough to support each "Prophet" card. To use as a teaching tool, scramble the cards on a metal tray, then try to put them back in the proper sequence.

Label an envelope with the word *Prophets* and store the cards in it. Use the game pieces at home on a tray, metal cabinet, or refrigerator. If desired, make magnetic cards for the remaining forty-nine books of the Bible and add them to the game.

NAIL BOARD PUZZLE

METHOD

Although it's easy to find the first book of the Bible—Genesis—it's also helpful to learn how to locate all sixty-six books in God's Word. Make a nail board puzzle and use it to review the names of the books of the Bible and to study the order in which they have been placed in Scripture.

Select a board to use for the project. Sand the wood to smooth the rough edges. Cover the board with a coat of paint and set it aside to dry.

Photocopy and cut apart the Bible cards on pages 76–79. You will not need the card labeled "We learn God's faithfulness in the Book of _____" on page 79. Punch a hole in the top of each piece. Place the tags in an envelope. Label the envelope "Books of the Bible."

Once the painted board is dry, drive sixty-six nails into the wood until they are secure, but still protruding. Space the nails evenly across the board—for example, five rows of thirteen nails—with one row containing fourteen nails.

Now that the parts of the game are ready, hang the tags on the nails in the order in which the books are found in the Bible. "Genesis" should be on the first hook, and "Revelation" should be on the last. Once the task has been accomplished, return the tags to the envelope so the game may be played again.

MATERIALS

pages 76–79
Bible(s)
envelopes
hammers
markers
nails (66 per
  project)
paint
paintbrushes
paper punch
pens
sandpaper
scissors
wooden boards
  12 by 10 inch,
  or any size

STICK SEQUENCING GAME

METHOD

MATERIALS
Bible(s)
craft sticks
markers

Play a game of "Sticks" to learn the order, or sequence, of the sixty-six books of Scripture. Using the table of contents in the front of the Bible as a guide, print the name of each book on a separate craft stick. Color-code the sticks to make the game easier to play. Make a large red dot on one end of the sticks with the names of the Old Testament books, and a big blue dot on one end of the sticks with the names of the New Testament books. Continue colorcoding the sticks by placing a green dot on the game pieces containing the names of the books of the Law, an orange dot on the sticks listing the books of History, and so forth. Be sure the color for each category is distinct. Once the game pieces are completed, decide if all or part of them will be used at the same time. It might be fun to learn to put the books in each category in order, to sequence the Old Testament list, then the New Testament volumes, and finally to try all sixty-six at once.

To play the game, place the sticks in a can or box and "spill" them onto a flat surface. The object of the game is to put the sticks in sequence by picking up each piece without moving the other items in the pile. A successful player may continue until he or she picks up the name of the wrong book, or until the person disturbs the pile. Other players continue this pattern. The game ends when all of the sticks are face up in a row in the proper order.

TWO-PART PUZZLE

METHOD

MATERIALS
cardboard, cereal or shirt boxes, or 5- by 7-inch index cards
crayons or markers
manila envelope
scissors

Make two-part puzzles and use them to match the names and the numbers, or sequence, of the books of the Bible. Cut cardboard into five- or seven-inch pieces, or use five- by seven-inch index cards for the project. Draw a wiggly line down the center of each rectangle.

On the left side of each piece, write a number such as "1," and on the right side, print the name of the first book of the Bible. Continue until all books of the Old Testament, the New Testament, or the selected category of Scripture have been used. Last, cut each rectangle apart along the wiggly line to create a two-piece puzzle. Mix up the pieces and try putting them together by matching the number and the name in each pair. Store the set in a manila envelope.

"WHAT'S MISSING?" GAME

ADVANCE PREPARATION

Photocopy and cut apart the Bible names on pages 76–79. Omit the last column on page 79.

METHOD

"What's Missing?" is a fun game to play. Items are placed on a tray. The tray is shown to the group, players are challenged to remember the objects, and the tray is removed. One item is taken away, the tray is displayed again, and players must guess what's missing. In First Corinthians, Chapter 13, Paul reminds us of something that should never be missing—love. In fact, love is the theme of every book of the Bible. It's not missing from any of them.

Play "What's Missing?" as a way to remember Paul's great chapter on love, 1 Corinthians 13. Then use the same method to review the names, and the sequence, of the rest of the books of the Bible—all of which include the message of God's love!

Prepare a tray of miscellaneous objects, including the symbol of a heart, and show it to a small group or to the whole class. Give the participants twenty or thirty seconds to memorize the items. Remove the tray, or ask the players to close their eyes or to turn their backs. Take away the heart. Show the tray again and challenge the contestants to guess "What's Missing?" Ask the person who says "heart" to share this item's connection to the book of First Corinthians. Chapter thirteen is known as Paul's great message on love. Look up the passage in a Bible and read it aloud. Remember that the entire Bible—all sixty-six books— contains the story of God's love. Play the game again, only this time fill the tray with the pieces of paper containing the names of the books of the Bible. It might be easier to review one section of each Testament at a time. For example, for the category "Law," place five cards on the tray—Genesis, Exodus, Leviticus, Numbers, and Deuteronomy—and show it to the group. After the designated amount of time, remove the tray and take away one card. Display the tray again and ask the players to guess "What's Missing?" Continue until all categories of Scripture are reviewed. For an extra challenge at the end of the game, place all of the cards on the floor, then remove one, and ask the group to guess which book is missing. Once the game is completed, the sixty-six cards may be put in the order in which the books are contained in the Bible. Remember that God's love is never missing and that we are challenged to share love with others in all that we do.

MATERIALS

pages 76–79
Bible(s)
heart-shaped item
miscellaneous objects (10 to 20) such as a coin, an eraser, and a rubber band

Genesis	Judges	First Chronicles
Exodus	Ruth	Second Chronicles
Leviticus	First Samuel	Ezra
Numbers	Second Samuel	Nehemiah
Deuteronomy	First Kings	Esther
Joshua	Second Kings	Job

Psalms	Lamentations	Obadiah
Proverbs	Ezekiel	Jonah
Ecclesiastes	Daniel	Micah
Song of Songs	Hosea	Nahum
Isaiah	Joel	Habakkuk
Jeremiah	Amos	Zephaniah

Haggai	John	Ephesians
Zechariah	Acts	Philippians
Malachi	Romans	Colossians
Matthew	First Corinthians	First Thessalonians
Mark	Second Corinthians	Second Thessalonians
Luke	Galatians	First Timothy

Second Timothy	Second Peter	We learn God's faithfulness in the Book of _____
Titus	First John	
Philemon	Second John	Old Testament
Hebrews	Third John	New Testament
James	Jude	
First Peter	Revelation	

Epistles	Pauline	Pauline	Pauline	Pauline	Pauline
General					Pauline
General					Pauline
General					Pauline
General					Pauline
General					Pauline
General	General	General	Pauline	Pauline	Pauline

CLOTHESPIN GAME BOARD

Count out twenty-two clip clothespins.
Using a permanent marker, print the words
New Testament on one clothespin,
and letter the name of each epistle
on the remaining twenty-one.
Mix up the clothespins and place them
in a basket or box. Pick one clothespin
at a time and read the name of the book
that's written on it. First decide
if the book is a Pauline Epistle
or a General Epistle. Then clip the pin
to a square on the board, putting the books
in their proper New Testament sequence.
The "New Testament" clothespin should
be attached to the square labeled "Epistles."

TELLING THE STORY THROUGH MUSIC

Learn a song about an Old Testament person. Try an instrument that was mentioned in the Bible. Listen to a recording to introduce a lesson. Attend a performance of a children's choir from another country. Write new words to an old tune to express an idea. These are just some of the ways in which music can be used to teach a lesson and to tell a story.

From the songs of Miriam and Mary, the praise of the psalmists and Paul, to the hymns and choruses of the liturgy, the use of music is recorded throughout Scripture and church history as a way to help people express a wide range of human emotions. Today, music is used extensively in the worship, education, outreach, and nurture ministries of congregations. It is an art form and a teaching tool that is familiar to both the educator and the student. Since it is a participatory learning activity, it is a good method to use to involve children in the storytelling process.

Ten ideas for telling the story through music are provided. They include many themes and techniques. Use them to supplement and support learning in a variety of classroom settings.

ALLELUIA
METHOD

We make music in church because the Bible tells us we should, because historically the church has sung songs of faith, and because we need more than ordinary words to express our devotion to God. Explain that when a musician writes a musical score, he or she uses special marks called musical notes—sometimes eighth, quarter, half, or whole notes—to indicate what sounds are to be produced and how long those sounds should be held. When the music is written

MATERIALS
blank sheets of
  musical score
  paper
markers
guitarist,
  organist, or
  pianist

down, we can praise God together because we know which sound to make and how long to hold it.

Invite the participants to accent a simple word of praise, "Alleluia." Ask the children to choose four notes from A to G. Have a musician write the notes on a sheet of musical score paper. Then play and sing the new "Alleluia" together as an expression of praise to God. Continue the process until many "Alleluias" are produced.

BOTTLES

METHOD

Tell the group that they are going to create a musical scale by filling bottles with water. Then they will learn, or make up, a song to share the story of Jesus' baptism, recorded in Matthew 3:13-17.

To form the musical scale, gather eight clear, twenty-ounce glass or plastic bottles. Remove the labels. Wash and dry the containers. With a permanent marker, print a number on each bottle beginning with *1* and ending with *8*. Use a measuring cup to fill the bottles with the following proportions of water to create the major scale:

MATERIALS
Bibles
bottles, 8–20-
   ounce clear
   glass or plastic
   containers
chalk or marker
chalkboard,
   newsprint, or
   white board
measuring cups
plastic tubing
scissors
water
optional: dowel
   rods, food
   coloring

    1: Do, 7 ounces
    2: Re, 9.5 ounces
    3: Mi, 12.5 ounces
    4: Fa, 14 ounces
    5: Sol, 16.5 ounces
    6: La, 17.5 ounces
    7: Ti, 18.5 ounces
    8: Do, 19 ounces

If desired, add different hues of food coloring to each bottle.

Practice playing a simple water-related tune such as "Row, Row, Row Your Boat" on the bottle scale. Have the children take turns blowing across the lip of the bottles. In order to allow more participants to play the notes, and to keep the tops of the bottles sanitary, consider having each person use a piece of flexible plastic tubing to blow into the necks of the bottles to create the sound. Because blowing into the bottle causes the air to vibrate, the bottles with the most water in them will make the highest notes. As an alternative, tap each bottle with a dowel rod to cause the glass to vibrate and produce a sound. In this case, the water dampens the

vibrations, so the less water in the bottle, the lower the pitch.
The pattern for "Row, Row, Row Your Boat," whether blowing or
tapping, is:

1, 1, 1, 2, 3.
3, 2, 3, 4, 5.
8, 8, 8, 5, 5, 5, 3, 3, 3, 1, 1, 1.
5, 4, 3, 2, 1.

Invite the group to make up verses to share the story of Jesus'
baptism. When the compositions are created, ask one person to play
the music on the bottle scale and everyone else to sing the songs.

BELL

METHOD

Design a flower pot bell to ring in the season of Easter and to tell the
story of the good news of Jesus' resurrection.

Wash a terra cotta flower pot with a rag or a towel dipped into a mild
vinegar and water solution. This will clean away any mineral deposits
or dust on the clay surface. Allow the pot to dry before painting it.
Use acrylic craft paints and brushes of various sizes to decorate the
flower pot with symbols and words related to the Easter message. Be
sure to paint the pot upside down, not right side up. Print the word
Alleluia in several places on the flower pot and add illustrations
related to the theme of resurrection, especially flowers.

Thread two ends of cord or twine through the hole in a large bead or
through the holes in a large button. Tie a knot at the bottom of the
bead or button—allowing the ends of the cord to extend beyond the
knot. Tie the jingle bell onto the remaining cord. Pull the loop up
through the flower pot hole to form a hanger for the bell. The bead or
button and knot will allow the jingle bell to hang freely for a better
sound.

MATERIALS

acrylic paint,
 various colors
bead or button,
 large
cleanup supplies
cord or twine
jingle bell, large
paintbrushes
rag or towel
terra cotta flower
 pot
vinegar
water
marker

KAZOO

METHOD

"The Hallelujah Chorus," an oratorio from George Frederich Handel's masterpiece, *Messiah,* is based on texts from Revelation 11:15 and 19:6, 16. Handel's majestic music and radiant lyrics proclaim that "Jesus shall reign forever and ever." If possible, play a recording of this selection.

The Book of Revelation is filled with hymns. Chapters 4 and 5, especially, focus on praising God as holy (4) and Christ as Savior (5). Look up more verses and songs to God in different passages, familiar to children, such as: Matthew 19:13-14 (Jesus Loves Me); Matthew 6:9-13 (The Lord's Prayer); Psalm 72:19 (Blessed Be the Name); Psalm 118:24 (This Is the Day); and so on. Next, look in the back of a hymnal for references to words such as *faith, trust, heaven,* and *joy.*

Select at least one song that summarizes the point or meaning for the lesson. Construct a kazoo, and then play the music on the new instrument. To make the kazoo, use markers to decorate a cardboard tube. Wrap a piece of wax paper over one end of the tube. Secure the wax paper with a rubber band. Using the point of a scissors, carefully cut or poke two holes in the top of the tube. Space the holes out a bit so they're not right on top of one another. To play the kazoo, hum the song into the open end of the tube. Cover and uncover the two holes with the fingers to make different sounds. To create other interesting sounds, make kazoos with tubes that have different diameters, thicknesses, and lengths, such as a paper towel tube cut in half, or a long wrapping paper roll.

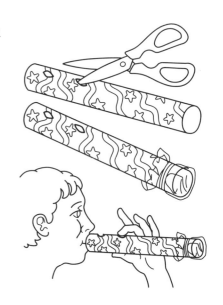

Practice the song and play the kazoo with others. Learn new hymns based on the theme of your lesson and hold a mini-concert as a way of sharing what the children have learned.

Bibles
cassette or CD
  player
hymnals
markers
cardboard tubes
recording of "The
  Hallelujah
  Chorus" from
  Handel's
  Messiah
rubber bands
scissors
wax paper
tape

HYMNS

METHOD

People from every country in the world use music to share their love for God. In recent years Christian hymnals and supplementary songbooks have included a variety of music from places other than Europe and the United States.

Challenge the children to look through books to find songs from various countries that highlight each season of the church year. For example, there was a dance tune in Malawi, Africa, that was turned into a Christmas carol called "That Boy-Child of Mary" by a Scottish missionary named Tom Colvin. Based on Malawi customs, the song celebrates the naming of the babe of Bethlehem and tells us why his name is so important—because *Jesus* means "Savior."

Refer to the eight books in the series *Hymn Stories for Children* by Phyllis Vos Wezeman and Anna L. Liechty—*Lent and Easter, Resources for Children's Worship, Special Days and Holidays, Spirituals, The Apostles' Creed, The Christmas Season, The Lord's Prayer*, and *The Ten Commandments*—for background information on many of these cultural songs.

MATERIALS
hymnals
Hymn Stories for Children

MOVEMENT

METHOD

Try playing musical chairs in a way that stresses cooperation rather than competition. Use background music that fits a biblical theme or topic. Explain that a chair will be removed each time the music stops, but no one will be eliminated from the game. Participants are to crowd onto the remaining seats. Watch the fun begin when only one chair remains, and all of the students attempt to get on it.

As an additional or an alternate activity, play a seated version of musical chairs to review the names and the sequence of the books of the Bible. While the pupils sit in a circle, play music and pass a Bible among the participants in a reverent and respectful manner. When the music stops, ask the person holding the Bible to name the first book of the Old Testament. The game continues in this manner until all sixty-six books are named. If a player does not know the answer, he or she may look it up in the table of contents.

MATERIALS
Bible(s)
chairs, one per
  person
cassette tapes or
  CDs of
  background
  music
CD or cassette
  player

PATTERN

METHOD

MATERIALS

music to "Jesus
   Loves the Little
   Children"
optional: globe or
   world map

Use the words of a hymn or a song as a pattern for a guided prayer. Sing a familiar chorus such as "Jesus Loves the Little Children" as a prayer that people around the world will hear—and believe—God's message of hope in their own lives. Ask the group to sing the first verse of the song.

Invite everyone to participate in a prayer in which he or she can remember children—as well as people of all ages—in all parts of the world. Sing the first two lines of the song again. Stop after the phrase "all the children of the world." Explain that each continent will be named—Africa, Antarctica, Asia, Australia, Europe, North America, and South America—and that a brief pause will follow each statement. Encourage the group to pray for the people of that particular region during the silence. Begin the song again, stop after the first two lines, and name each continent. Pause for silent prayer. Sing the remainder of the song and conclude with "Amen." Try the technique with additional songs such as "He's Got the Whole World in His Hands," "Kum Ba Ya," or "We Shall Overcome."

RECORDING

METHOD

MATERIALS

cassette tapes,
   blank
cassette tape
   players, two
cassette tapes or
   compact disks
   of music (in
   publc domain)
   to fit the
   selected Bible
   story or theme

Prepare a powerful musical message related to a Scripture story or a theological theme. Choose a topic such as cooperation, justice, or stewardship around which to center this creative communication.

Gather recordings of contemporary choruses, popular songs, and traditional hymns that are in public domain. Play some and listen carefully to the content. Choose phrases or lines that are meaningful and put them together to form a message related to the topic.

Play the selected segment and record it onto a blank cassette tape. Continue adding sections until the message is completed. Use a process such as: find the phrase to be recorded on the cassette tape or CD. Start playing the CD just before that point. When the CD reaches the chosen phrase, press the "record" button on the tape recorder. When the chosen phrase is over, press the tape recorder's stop button. Go on to another CD and repeat. The entire class may work on the project together, or it may be done individually. Allow the children to take turns sharing the message with their own families, or set up a special display or demonstration so families of the church may hear it.

SHOFAR

METHOD

Sound the shofar as a way to call people to action or to make a connection with a biblical story or subject. Show the children an example or a picture of a shofar, an instrument made of a ram's horn. The ram's horn serves as a reminder of the Hebrew scripture story, recorded in Genesis 22, in which Abraham substituted a ram as a sacrifice in place of his son, Isaac. Originally, the shofar was used as a way to send messages from one hillside to another. It signaled the need for immediate action, such as in the case of attack or fire. The shofar was also used as a trumpet in battle.

Sounding the shofar consists of making a set of sounds repeated three times, followed by a longer sound. Hebrew words are spoken to describe the sounds. Today the shofar is sounded at the time of the highest Jewish holidays, Rosh Hashanah and Yom Kipper, to herald a need for action.

Invite the group to make simple shofars from paper plates. Place the supplies within sharing distance of the participants. Instruct the learners to cut a shofar shape from a paper plate. They may use patterns or create the design freehand. Tell them to turn the shape over and to trace it on another paper plate. Cut it out. Place the two shapes together to form a shofar. Using a paper punch, make evenly spaced holes along the two sides of the ram's horn shape. With yarn, string, shoelaces, or lacing cord, sew the two pieces together.

As the children work, play a recording that features a shofar, if you have access to one.

Use the shofar to illustrate an Old Testament story, such as Joshua and the walls of Jericho, or to teach about the Jewish holidays.

MATERIALS
Bible(s)
paper punch
lacing cord,
  shoelaces,
  string, or yarn
markers
paper plates, two
  per person
scissors
shofar (or picture)
optional:
  recording of
  shofar sounds
  and equipment
  to play it

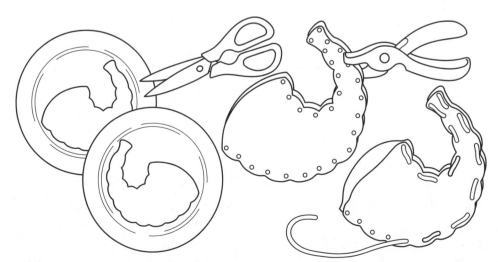

WORDS

Bibles
chalk or markers
chalkboard or
  newsprint
formula for
  quatrain poetry
paper
pencils or pens

METHOD

The book of Job tells the story of a man named Job. Since most of it is in poetic form, use a quatrain formula to write one or more verses to tell this interesting and important story. Quatrains are four-line poems that follow any one of four different rhyme patterns: AABB; ABAB; ABBA; ABCB. When quatrains are combined to form one long poem, each group of four lines is called a stanza. Stanzas are the paragraphs of poetry. Quatrains are often used in songs called ballads. Write a quatrain poem to learn more about the story of Job. Each person may write one or more stanzas to tell the story, or portions of Scripture may be assigned to individuals or small groups and combined to form one long ballad.

Write the poetry patterns on a chalkboard or on newsprint. Remember that the lines with the same letters rhyme with each other. For example, in the formula AABB, the first two lines rhyme with each other, and the last two lines rhyme as well. Using the pattern ABAB, lines one and three rhyme, and lines two and four rhyme. Have each person or pair select a quatrain formula and a piece of paper, plus a pencil or pen. Review the story of Job in the Bible and write verses to share the information. For example, using an ABCB pattern:

> Job was a man who loved the Lord.
> He had family, friends, and fame,
> If it's all taken away from him,
> Do you think he'll ignore God's name?

Once the verses are completed, compose or find a tune to fit the words. Sing the stanzas to review the story.

TELLING THE STORY THROUGH PUPPETRY

What do plastic bottles, paper bags, newspapers, cardboard egg cartons, and aluminum cans have to do with Old Testament heroes and heroines, New Testament stories, and Christian themes? They all relate to puppets! Puppetry is the art of bringing an inanimate object to life and communicating a thought, theme, or topic with it. Puppets are used in congregations in worship, education, outreach, and nurture ministries. They make announcements, play roles during children's sermons, illustrate songs, teach Sunday school lessons, highlight seasonal programs, visit nursing homes, and much more.

Ideas for the ten projects in this chapter focus on puppets that can be quickly and easily constructed from low-cost or no-cost, readily available items. Six basic puppet styles—body, finger, hand, marionette, rod, and shadow—are represented in the examples. Generally speaking, puppets are operated by a person's fingers, hands, or body, or by strings or rods. A body puppet is worn on the body of the operator and worked by the movement of the wearer. A finger puppet is placed on a person's finger(s), with movement achieved when individual fingers indicate action. A hand puppet is worn on the person's hand, much like a glove or a mitten, and operated by the movement of the fingers, hand, wrist, and arm. A marionette is worked on strings that are attached to various parts of the puppet's body and to a control bar operated by the puppeteer. A rod puppet contains a central stick in the body that forms the basis for construction and manipulation. A shadow puppet is cut from paper or carved from wood, operated with rods, and pressed against a screen with a light source behind it to project a silhouette to the audience.

Try any or all of the suggestions to tell Bible stories and to teach religious themes and topics.

BROOM ROD PUPPET

MATERIALS

brooms, any size
fabric or plastic
  bags
felt
glue
scissors
tape
double-sided tape

METHOD

Begin with a broom and end with a puppet that can help to teach a passage such as the parable of the lost coin. Turn a broom of any size upside down. The bristles become the head of the puppet, and the handle forms the body. Cut eyes, nose, and mouth from felt scraps. Glue them to one side of the bristles or secure them in place with small pieces of double-sided tape.

Make a costume by slitting the center of a piece of fabric or plastic bag. Slide it up the handle and tape it at the neck of the character. Hold the puppet by the handle to operate it.

CARDBOARD EGG CARTON FINGER PUPPET

MATERIALS

cardboard egg
  cartons
construction
  paper
glue
markers
scissors
yarn
straw

METHOD

Use a cardboard egg carton to make finger puppets representing the characters mentioned in a Bible story, such as the Genesis 1 and 2 account of Creation or the Gospel lists of the twelve disciples.

Cut the egg cups from the carton and use each of them for a puppet head. Cut two holes in the top of each egg cup. Show the children how to place the egg cup hole-side down. Eyes, nose, and mouth may be drawn on with marker, or cut from construction paper scraps and glued into place. Ears can be cut from paper and glued onto the side. Make hair from yarn and attach it to the top. Straw could be used for whiskers. Try to make each character look unique. Show the children how to insert their first two fingers in the holes at the bottom so the puppet has legs.

CLOTH-COVERED HAND PUPPET

METHOD

Make a puppet to represent each character mentioned in a Scripture passage, such as one of Jesus' miracle stories. To form the head, cut or poke a hole in the bottom of a plastic foam ball so that it will comfortably fit the index finger. Create a face on the puppet's head by drawing features with markers or by cutting them from felt or paper and gluing them in place.

Form a puppet body by covering one hand with a fifteen-inch cloth square, scarf, or handkerchief. Place the puppet head on the index finger. Put one rubber band around the thumb and another around the middle finger to hold the costume in place.

Review the story in a "Round Robin" format. Each person, in turn, will have an opportunity to add five words to a story and will use the puppet to tell the story.

MATERIALS
cloth squares,
  scarfs, or
  handkerchiefs
glue
markers
rubber bands
scissors
plastic foam balls
felt or paper

CUP HAND PUPPET

METHOD

Salvage paper or plastic foam cups and turn them into puppets. The bottom of the cup becomes the top of the puppet. Use a pen or permanent marker to design a face on one side of the cup. Draw a circle for the nose. With scissors, carefully cut out the circle. Create a bundle of tied yarn for hair and glue it to the top of the puppet. Fabric may be glued to the rim of the cup to form a costume. To use the puppet, insert one hand into the cup. Project the index or middle finger through the hole to form a nose. Use the cup puppet to tell a first-person story about the life of an Old Testament person such as Abraham or Sarah or a New Testament person such as Elizabeth or Zechariah.

MATERIALS
fabric
glue
paper or plastic
  foam cups
pens or
  permanent
  markers,
  various colors
scissors
yarn

ENVELOPE HAND PUPPET

METHOD

MATERIALS

envelopes, any
  size
fabric,
  construction
  paper, or plastic
  bags
glue
markers
scissors
yarn

Choose an envelope to make into a person puppet. Tuck the flap inside the envelope. Place one hand inside the envelope. The thumb should touch the bottom corner, and four fingers should extend towards the top corner. Use the other hand to press on the bottom crease, between the thumb and the fingers, and bring the two lower corners of the envelope together. This will form a moveable mouth. Use markers or scraps of construction paper to add eyes and a nose to the face. Make hair by cutting strips of yarn and gluing them to the top of the head. Create a costume by cutting a piece of fabric, construction paper, or plastic bag and gluing it to the edges of the envelope.

Use the envelope puppets to give summary reports of Paul's letters, or epistles, to the early Christians. Assign each of Paul's New Testament writings to a different individual or small group, and ask participants to summarize its message. Have the envelope puppets share this information with the whole class. Also, use the puppets to encourage people to write letters to missionaries supported by the congregation.

GIANT GARBAGE BAG ROD PUPPET

METHOD

MATERIALS

cardboard pole
  from carpet or
  fabric
construction
  paper or paper
  plates
duct tape
disposable
  packaging and
  products
fabric, packing
  material, or
  plastic bags
newspaper
plastic garbage
  bags, large
yarn
scissors

Form giant puppets from throwaway materials to illustrate Bible stories such as David and Goliath from the Old Testament or the three wise men from the New Testament. Each puppet will be easier to make if several people, or teams, work on the project.

Form the head of the puppet from a large plastic garbage bag. To make it stronger, use several bags inside of one another. Hold open the bag(s). Gather the throwaway materials. Unfold the newspaper and stack it in a pile. Crumple the newspaper, one sheet at a time, and stuff it into the open bag. It is important to crumple it one sheet at a time, as the puppet head will become too lumpy if several sheets are used together. Fill the bag with the remaining materials. Be sure the weight is distributed as evenly as possible. When the bag is approximately half full, insert the pole into the middle of the disposable items. Continue stuffing the bag. When the bag is full, gather the top of it around the pole and tape it securely. Turn the puppet upside down. Continue to hold the puppet while the features and costume are added.

Make rolls of duct tape to use to stick the features to the puppet. Cut two eyes from construction paper or paper plates and attach them to the face. Cut a nose, ears, and a mouth and affix them to the head. Make hair from yarn or another material and attach it to the top of the stuffed bag.

Construct a simple costume from packaging material, bags, or lightweight fabric, such as an old sheet. Snip a hole in the center of the piece, and slide it up the pole. Tape the costume into place around the neck of the puppet. Trim with additional scraps to create the desired effect. Use the cardboard pole to carry and operate the puppet.

PAPER AND PLASTIC BAG BODY PUPPET

METHOD

It's easy to recycle paper and plastic bags into body puppets. This type of puppet is worn, rather than held, to operate it. Using any Bible story, choose the characters to create.

Start with a brown paper grocery bag. The bottom flap of it will become the puppet's head, and the remainder of the bag will be the body. Pick a full sheet of construction paper and glue it to the body portion of the bag. Make a face on the flap. Decorate the character with markers and additional construction paper.

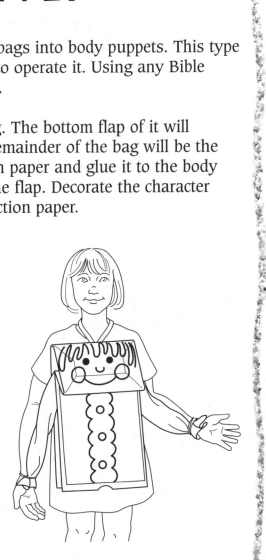

Make a neck strap by cutting a 30- by 2-inch piece of yarn. Staple the center of the yarn to the middle of the top of the bag. For arms, cut two 18- by 2-inch strips of plastic bag. Tie a rubber band to the end of each piece of plastic. Staple the other end of each arm strip to the plastic bag, just below the flap.

To wear and work the puppet, tie the yarn around the puppeteer's neck, and slip the rubber bands over his or her wrists. The puppeteer's motions and movements manipulate the puppet.

MATERIALS

brown paper
  grocery bags
construction
  paper
glue
markers
plastic bags
rubber bands,
  medium, two
  per puppet
scissors
stapler and
  staples
yarn

PAPER BAG MARIONETTE

METHOD

crayons or markers
glue
needles with
   large eyes
newspapers
paper grocery
   bags, one per
   puppet
lunch-size paper
   bags, five per
   puppet
scissors
stapler, staples
string
wood strips, 1 by
   4 by 3/8; and 1
   by 14 by 3/8
CD or cassette
   recording of
   "Dry Bones"
optional:
   hammer, nails,
   illustration of
   bones of the
   human body

Make one or more paper bag marionette people to use to tell a story such as Ezekiel and the dry bones. The large grocery bag will be the body of the puppet, and the five paper lunch bags become the head, arms, and legs.

Begin by using crayons or markers and drawing a face on one side of one of the lunch bags. Open the five small bags. Crumple individual sheets of newspaper and stuff each bag half full of newspaper. Fold over the tops of the bags and staple them shut. Staple the face to the center of the top of the closed grocery bag. Attach two of the stuffed bags to the bottom of the large piece to form the legs and the others to each side of the top of the bag to make the arms. Draw bones on various parts of the body.

Make a control stick for the puppet by gluing or nailing the four-inch wood strip to the fourteen-inch wood strip. The piece should resemble the letter *T*. Thread lengths of string through the arms and head of the puppet. Join the control bar to the strings. Attach the arm strings to the ends of the longer stick and the head control string to the shorter stick. Practice operating the marionette and learning how to make it look like it is walking and talking. Obtain music for the song "Dry Bones." Play or sing the familiar spiritual, and move the puppets to correspond with the lyrics.

PAPIER MACHE BALLOON ROD PUPPET

METHOD

Begin with a balloon, add papier mache, and create a puppet. Blow up a large, round balloon, and tie the end of it. Tear the newspaper into strips. Mix one cup of paste into ten cups of warm water. Stir until it is well blended. Dip the newspaper pieces into the paste and cover the balloon with two single layers of it. Make eyes, nose, mouth, ears, wrinkles, and other facial features by gluing cardboard strips, pieces of egg carton, or other materials to the face. Cover the head with two more layers of the paste-covered paper.

While the head is drying, carefully insert a dowel rod into the center of the bottom of the puppet. This will be the handle by which the puppet is operated.

After the puppet head is dry, paint the head with tempera paints. Make hair from yarn, cotton, fake fur, feathers, paper curls, garland, or another material. Add a simple costume by sliding a piece of fabric up the rod and taping in into place.

Use the puppet to present a news report on the events that took place on a special occasion. Use some of the puppets as reporters and the rest as the people they interview. Tape record the various accounts, such as Pentecost, and play them back while the puppets portray the action.

Note of Caution: Do not pour papier mache paste into any drain.

MATERIALS

balloons
tape
large round bowl
  or bucket
cardboard strips
dowel rods
egg cartons
fabric
glue
newspaper
paint
paintbrushes
scissors
spoon or stirrer
water
wheat or
  wallpaper paste
yarn and materials
  for hair

POSTERBOARD SHADOW PUPPET

cellophane,
  various colors
masking tape
paper punch
posterboard,
  black
scissors
straws
paper, white
cardboard box
ruler
optional: light
  source, shadow
  puppet screen

METHOD

Silhouettes, cut from paper or carved from wood, that are operated with rods form shadow puppets. When this type of puppet is pressed against a screen with a light source behind it, a shadow projects to the audience. Shadow puppets are an excellent media to use to tell a story.

Cut the shape of a person or an object named in the story. Irregularly shaped, rather than square or rectangular, pieces of posterboard often spark creativity and imagination when working on a shadow puppet project. Add detail and decoration to the figures by cutting intricate and interesting designs into the paper to highlight features. A paper punch is helpful for this purpose. Tape pieces of colored cellophane behind some of the cut-out areas.

Form the rod by which the shadow figure is operated by taping the top inch, or bendable portion, of a straw to the center of the puppet. This should be placed on the back side. Try the puppet behind a shadow screen.

Make or set up a shadow puppet screen and light source. To construct a simple shadow puppet screen, cut the flaps off the top of a medium-sized cardboard box. Turn the box bottom up. Leaving a three-inch border around the edges, cut out the center of the bottom. The border helps to support the box. Working from the inside of the box, cover the opening just created with white paper. Tape it in place. Light the shadow puppet screen from behind with a light bulb, slide, or overhead projector, or with natural light from a window.

Take turns holding shadow puppets made by other people so that each participant has an opportunity to view his or her own work from the front, rather than the back of the screen.